1

Table of Contents

2

3

4

5

6

CHAPTER 1: Introduction to Large Language Models (LLMs)

Large Language Models (LLMs) are revolutionary tools that mimic human language capabilities, allowing computers to understand and generate text with remarkable accuracy. Imagine a computer that can converse fluently, analyze texts like a human, and even create original content—these models bring such possibilities closer every day. This eBook will guide you through the process of understanding, training, and deploying your own LLMs, equipping you with the knowledge and skills to leverage this powerful technology.

1.1 What Are Large Language Models? (The Magic Behind the Machine)

Large Language Models (LLMs) are advanced AI systems designed to interact with humans through language. But what exactly are they? Think of them as incredibly sophisticated pattern-matching machines. They process vast amounts of text, learning statistical relationships between words and phrases. This learning

9

allows them to perform tasks like translation, question answering, text summarization, and even creative writing.

Diving deeper, at their core, LLMs are built on neural networks, specifically transformer networks. These networks are designed to handle sequential data, like text, very efficiently. They use a mechanism called "attention" to focus on the most relevant parts of the input when generating the output. We'll delve into the details of transformers later, but for now, just remember that they are the engine that drives the LLM.

Imagine learning a new language by reading hundreds of books. You start to pick up on patterns in grammar and vocabulary, and eventually, you can understand and speak the language yourself. LLMs do something similar, but on a much larger scale and at incredible speed.

There are a few key concepts to understand when it comes to LLMs. They don't work with whole words; instead, they break text down into smaller units called

10

tokens. A token can be a word, a part of a word, or even a punctuation mark. Parameters are the adjustable weights in the neural network that the model learns during training. The number of parameters is often used as a measure of the model's size and complexity. The initial training phase, called pre-training, involves exposing the LLM to a massive dataset of text. Fine-tuning is the process of adapting a pre-trained LLM to a specific task by training it on a smaller, task-specific dataset.

By understanding these concepts, you'll gain a deeper appreciation for the magic behind the machine, and how LLMs are transforming the way we interact with technology.

1.2 A Brief History of LLM Development (From Humble Beginnings to AI Giants)

The journey of Large Language Models (LLMs) began in the 1950s, with early attempts laying the groundwork for modern capabilities. It's a fascinating story of innovation, with each breakthrough building upon the previous one.

11

In the early days of the 1950s to the 1970s, natural language processing (NLP) relied on rule-based systems. These systems used hand-crafted rules and dictionaries. While they could handle simple tasks, they were brittle and couldn't cope with the complexity of human language. Finite State Machines were introduced to understand basic language structures.

From the 1980s to the 2000s, statistical NLP methods and machine learning algorithms like Hidden Markov Models (HMMs) and Support Vector Machines (SVMs) emerged. These approaches allowed computers to learn from data rather than relying on explicit rules. Although this was a significant step forward, these models were still limited in their ability to understand and generate complex text.

In 2008, a breakthrough experiment demonstrated question-answering abilities using datasets designed for this purpose. This showcased the potential of data-driven approaches and marked a shift towards more interactive and context-aware systems.

The 2010s saw the advent of deep learning, particularly with recurrent neural networks (RNNs) like Long Short-Term Memory (LSTM) networks. These models enabled the capture of long-range dependencies in text, leading to significant improvements in machine translation and other NLP tasks.

In 2015, the Transformer model revolutionized translation by efficiently handling sequential data and reducing computational complexity. Unlike previous models that processed text sequentially, Transformers process entire sequences in parallel, making them much faster and more scalable. This was a game-changer.

From 2018 to the present, the rise of LLMs has been fueled by the Transformer architecture. Models like BERT and GPT are pre-trained on massive datasets of text and can be fine-tuned for a wide range of tasks. They have achieved state-of-the-art results on many NLP benchmarks and are transforming the way we interact with computers.

13

Key milestones in the development of LLMs include BERT in 2018, which introduced bidirectional training to consider both left and right context; GPT-2 in 2019, which demonstrated impressive text generation capabilities; GPT-3 in 2020, a massive model with 175 billion parameters capable of performing a wide range of tasks with little or no fine-tuning; and LaMDA in 2022, which showed remarkable conversational abilities designed for dialogue applications.

Each milestone marked a leap forward, transforming how we interact with digital tools and pushing the boundaries of what is possible in natural language processing.

1.3 Transforming AI and Society (LLMs in the Real World)

Large Language Models (LLMs) are reshaping industries across the board, and their impact is set to grow in the coming years. Here's a look at how they are being used today.

14

In healthcare, LLMs assist in diagnoses by analyzing symptoms and medical texts, aiding in treatment plans that consider multiple factors. They also accelerate drug discovery by analyzing research papers and identifying potential drug candidates. Additionally, LLMs help with patient education by providing personalized information about conditions and treatments.

In education, LLMs personalize learning experiences through adaptive content and provide instant feedback for a tailored educational journey. They also generate educational materials such as quizzes and summaries, and help students with research by summarizing articles and identifying relevant sources.

In the entertainment industry, LLMs craft personalized songs or movies that resonate with users, enhancing storytelling capabilities. They create interactive narratives where the story evolves based on the user's choices, and generate realistic dialogue for video games and virtual reality experiences.

15

In business, LLMs automate customer service via chatbots and analyze market trends to offer informed decisions. They generate marketing copy, translate documents, and summarize business reports, saving time and resources.

In finance, LLMs analyze financial data, detect fraud, and provide investment recommendations. They process vast amounts of financial information and identify patterns that humans might miss.

In the legal field, LLMs analyze legal documents, draft contracts, and conduct legal research, helping lawyers save time and improve accuracy.

These models drive innovations that profoundly impact our daily lives. As LLMs continue to evolve, their applications across various domains will expand, further integrating into our daily routines and transforming industries. Understanding their current and potential uses is key to harnessing their power for future developments.

1.4 Training LLMs (Feeding the Beast – Data and Compute)

The effectiveness of an LLM hinges on high-quality data. Consider a model trained mainly on fiction texts; when asked about non-fiction, it might struggle without sufficient context. Diverse datasets ensure broader understanding and applicability across various domains. This section will provide a brief overview of what's involved in training, with a deeper dive coming later.

Data, Data, Data: LLMs are trained on massive datasets of text. These datasets can include books, articles, websites, code, and more. The more diverse and comprehensive the dataset, the better the LLM will perform. Think of it like this: a student who has read a wide variety of books is likely to be more knowledgeable and articulate than a student who has only read a few books.

The Training Process: The training process involves feeding the LLM the text data and adjusting the model's parameters to minimize the difference between its

17

predictions and the actual text. This is a computationally intensive process that requires specialized hardware like GPUs. We'll get into the specifics of hardware requirements in later chapters.

Pre-training vs. Fine-tuning: As mentioned earlier, LLMs are typically pre-trained on a massive dataset and then fine-tuned for a specific task. Pre-training teaches the model general language skills, while fine-tuning adapts it to a particular domain or application.

Challenges of Training: Training LLMs can be challenging due to the massive size of the models and datasets involved. It requires significant computational resources, expertise, and careful monitoring to ensure the model is learning effectively.

1.5 Practical Tips for Understanding LLMs (A Few Key Takeaways)

Before diving deeper into the nuts and bolts of training, here are a few practical tips to keep in mind.

18

Hardware considerations are crucial. More powerful hardware, such as GPUs, accelerates processing. Think of how multiple apps run smoothly on a smartphone—it's similar to how LLMs process information quickly. You'll need serious computing power, so start thinking about GPUs and cloud computing options.

Data quality is another key factor. Ensure your training data is diverse and relevant. For instance, if a model excels in creative writing but lacks domain knowledge about specific fields, its outputs may be limited. Remember, "garbage in, garbage out."

When starting out, don't try to build the next GPT-3 on your first try. Begin with a smaller model and a smaller dataset to get a feel for the process. Learn to walk before you run.

Experimentation is important. There are many different LLM architectures and training techniques. Don't be afraid to experiment and see what works best for your specific needs. There's no one-size-fits-all solution.

Stay up-to-date in the field. The landscape of LLMs is rapidly evolving. Stay informed on the latest research and developments by reading research papers, attending conferences, and following experts in the field. Continuous learning is essential.

As we continue exploring, it's clear that these models have already started transforming industries, from healthcare to entertainment. They hold immense potential for future developments that will further integrate into our daily lives. LLMs are not just a technological advancement; they represent a paradigm shift in how we interact with computers and information. They enable us to automate tasks, generate creative content, and gain insights from vast amounts of data.

Stay tuned as LLMs unlock new possibilities, shaping the future of technology and society. The journey to mastering LLMs can be daunting, but with the right knowledge and tools, you can harness their power to build innovative applications that solve real-world problems. In the following chapters, we'll delve into the

20

practical aspects of training and deploying LLMs, providing you with the skills and expertise needed to succeed.

21

CHAPTER 2: The Hardware Foundation: Building the Infrastructure for LLM Success

Large Language Models (LLMs) are complex systems that require significant computational resources for effective training. Training an LLM involves processing vast amounts of text data, performing intricate mathematical computations, and optimizing model parameters to improve accuracy and performance. The hardware used for this task must be capable of handling these demanding operations efficiently.

This chapter provides a detailed understanding of the hardware requirements necessary for training LLMs. We will explore the key components involved, their functionalities, and their essential nature. We'll move beyond simple descriptions to offer concrete advice on selecting and configuring the optimal hardware for your specific LLM training needs.

2.1 The Power Behind Large Language Model (LLM) Training: GPUs, TPUs, and Beyond

Creating a Large Language Model (LLM) is an incredibly intensive task, requiring processing power far beyond most other computing tasks. This necessitates specialized hardware and carefully crafted algorithmic

22

strategies. Here's a look at the hardware and techniques that make LLM training possible and how they work together to transform raw data into sophisticated language-understanding machines.

The rise of specialized hardware has been a game-changer in this field. General-purpose CPUs, while versatile, are not optimized for the massively parallel computations required by deep learning. This has led to the development and adoption of specialized hardware accelerators.

Graphics Processing Units (GPUs), originally designed for rendering graphics in video games, have proven remarkably well-suited for deep learning due to their massively parallel architecture. They can perform thousands of calculations simultaneously, significantly accelerating the training process. GPUs have become the dominant choice for LLM training, offering a good balance of performance, cost, and accessibility. Their high memory bandwidth allows for rapid data transfer between the GPU and memory, and their large number of cores enables parallel processing of large batches of

23

data. Optimized libraries like CUDA (NVIDIA) provide routines for deep learning operations.

Tensor Processing Units (TPUs) were developed by Google specifically for machine learning. These custom-designed ASICs (Application-Specific Integrated Circuits) provide even greater performance than GPUs for certain workloads, especially those involving tensor operations, the fundamental building blocks of neural networks. TPUs offer higher throughput, improved energy efficiency, and tight integration with the TensorFlow framework.

Emerging hardware solutions are also making their mark. Field-Programmable Gate Arrays (FPGAs) offer a flexible and customizable hardware platform tailored to specific deep learning tasks. Neuromorphic computing, inspired by the structure and function of the human brain, offers a fundamentally different approach to computation that may be well-suited for certain AI workloads.

24

Scaling and distributed training often require distributing the workload across multiple machines. Data parallelism involves dividing the training data across multiple GPUs or TPUs, each of which trains a copy of the model. Model parallelism divides the model itself across multiple devices when it is too large to fit on a single GPU or TPU. Hybrid parallelism combines data and model parallelism to achieve optimal performance.

High-speed interconnects are crucial for efficient communication between GPUs or TPUs in a distributed training setup. These interconnects allow for rapid exchange of gradients and other data during the training process. Examples include NVLink (NVIDIA), a high-bandwidth interconnect specifically designed for connecting NVIDIA GPUs, and InfiniBand, a high-performance networking technology often used in high-performance computing clusters.

The choice of hardware and training algorithms are intertwined. Certain algorithms may be better suited for specific types of hardware, and vice versa.

25

Researchers are constantly exploring new hardware-algorithm co-design strategies to optimize performance and efficiency.

Training LLMs involves a complex interplay of powerful hardware, sophisticated algorithms, and advanced techniques for scaling and distributing the workload. The ongoing development of specialized hardware and improved training methods is enabling the creation of ever-larger and more capable language models, pushing the boundaries of what is possible in natural language processing. The "power behind language model training" isn't just about raw computational muscle; it's about intelligently leveraging that muscle with innovative hardware and algorithmic solutions.

2.2 The Role of GPUs: Accelerating Performance

Graphical Processing Units (GPUs) are pivotal in transforming the training landscape for Large Language Models (LLMs). These specialized chips are designed to handle data-parallel operations, which are crucial for processing large datasets efficiently. GPUs excel at

26

performing the same operation on many data points simultaneously, which is exactly what's needed for the matrix multiplications at the heart of deep learning. They are readily available, well-supported by deep learning frameworks, and relatively cost-effective, especially for smaller projects compared to TPUs.

When selecting a GPU for LLM training, there are several important specifications to consider. Memory, or VRAM, is crucial for fitting the model and intermediate calculations. A 24GB GPU will allow for larger batch sizes and more complex models than an 8GB GPU. For modern LLMs, aim for at least 16GB, and preferably 24GB or more. Compute power, measured in TFLOPS, indicates the GPU's ability to perform floating-point operations. Higher TFLOPS means faster training. The interconnect, such as NVLink or PCIe, is critical if using multiple GPUs. NVLink (NVIDIA) provides much faster communication than PCIe but is only available on certain high-end GPUs.

For instance, the NVIDIA A100 with 40GB or 80GB of HBM2e memory is a popular choice for LLM training,

27

offering excellent performance and scalability. A more budget-friendly option is the NVIDIA RTX 3090 or RTX 4090, though they have less memory and slower interconnects.

Before buying a GPU, check its compatibility with your chosen deep learning framework, such as TensorFlow or PyTorch. Ensuring compatibility will help you make the most of your hardware's capabilities, leading to more efficient and effective training processes. By understanding the role and specifications of GPUs, you can make informed decisions that enhance the performance of your LLM training.

2.3 The Vision of TPUs: Tailored for Language Models

Tensor Processing Units (TPUs) are custom-made chips specifically designed for machine learning tasks. Built from the ground up to handle tensor operations—fundamental to deep learning computations—TPUs are highly efficient at performing these calculations at a much faster pace than traditional GPUs.

28

TPUs are like Google's secret weapon in the world of deep learning. They are designed specifically for the types of computations common in this field, excelling at matrix multiplications and other tensor operations. This specialization allows TPUs to deliver exceptional performance for machine learning tasks.

In terms of availability and cost, TPUs are primarily accessible through the Google Cloud Platform (GCP). While they offer significant performance advantages, they can also be more expensive than GPUs, making them a less practical choice for smaller projects.

For very large LLM training runs, Google offers TPU Pods, which consist of hundreds or even thousands of interconnected TPUs. These TPU Pods provide a powerful infrastructure for handling extensive training tasks.

When deciding whether to use TPUs, consider the size of your project and your access to GCP. TPUs can be a good option if you are training a very large LLM and need the performance benefits they offer. However, for smaller projects, GPUs are often a more practical and cost-effective choice.

A practical tip is to experiment with both GPUs and TPUs to see which performs better for your specific workload. Google Colab offers free access to TPUs, allowing you to test them out without incurring significant costs. This approach can help you make an informed decision about the best hardware for your machine learning tasks.

2.4 Cloud Computing: A Flexible Framework

Training a large language model (LLM) can be resource-intensive, requiring access to scalable computing environments. Cloud computing provides a flexible framework that allows you to allocate resources as needed.

One of the major benefits of cloud computing is scalability. This allows you to easily scale up or down your resources as needed, ensuring that you always have the right amount of computational power. Cloud

30

computing is also cost-effective, as you only pay for the resources you use, which can help manage expenses.

Another advantage is accessibility. Cloud computing enables you to access powerful hardware from anywhere in the world, making it convenient to manage and run your training processes. Additionally, cloud providers offer managed infrastructure, handling the maintenance and management of the hardware so you can focus on your training tasks.

Several popular cloud providers offer robust services for machine learning. Amazon Web Services (AWS) provides a wide range of GPU instances, including NVIDIA A100 and V100. Google Cloud Platform (GCP) offers TPUs and GPUs, as well as managed services for machine learning. Microsoft Azure also offers NVIDIA GPUs and a comprehensive set of AI services.

When choosing a cloud provider, it's important to compare the pricing and performance of different options. Consider using spot instances (AWS) or preemptible VMs (GCP) to reduce costs. However, be aware that these instances can be terminated with little notice, so plan accordingly.

By leveraging cloud computing, you can create a flexible and scalable environment for training your LLM, optimizing both performance and cost-effectiveness.

2.5 Storage Solutions: Organizing Data Efficiently

Data storage is a crucial component in training large language models (LLMs). Efficiently managing and storing data is essential for smooth operations during the training process.

Speed is a significant factor, as LLMs require rapid access to vast amounts of data. Slow storage can become a bottleneck, significantly hindering the training process. To address this, various storage options can be utilized based on their speed and suitability.

NVMe SSDs are the fastest type of storage available and are ideal for storing the training dataset. They provide quick access to data, which is essential for efficient

32

training. SATA SSDs, although slower than NVMe SSDs, are still much faster than traditional hard disk drives (HDDs) and can be a viable option for slightly less critical data storage needs. HDDs, on the other hand, are suitable for storing less frequently accessed data, such as backups and archival information.

A practical tip for efficient storage management is to use a tiered storage system. This system stores the most frequently accessed data on the fastest storage devices, ensuring that the critical data needed for training is quickly accessible.

In addition to local storage options, cloud storage offers various solutions for data management. Providers like Amazon S3, Google Cloud Storage, and Azure Blob Storage offer highly scalable and durable storage services. However, it's important to consider that cloud storage can be more expensive than local storage.

By understanding and implementing these storage solutions, you can organize your data efficiently, ensuring that your LLM training process runs smoothly and effectively. This approach helps to optimize data access and improve overall training performance.

2.6 Power Management: Ensuring Smooth Operation

Ensuring a reliable power supply is fundamental to any machine learning setup, especially for training large language models (LLMs). These models require a steady and robust power source to function optimally.

High-performance GPUs and TPUs, which are often used in LLM training, consume a significant amount of power. It's crucial to ensure that your power supply can handle this load. An adequate power supply unit (PSU) is essential. You should choose a PSU with enough wattage to power all your components comfortably, leaving some headroom for future expansion. High-quality PSUs also provide more stable power, enhancing the reliability of your system.

Monitoring power consumption is another important aspect of power management. Using a power meter can help you track the power usage of your system,

34

allowing you to identify potential problems and optimize your power consumption.

For more precise monitoring and control, consider using a power distribution unit (PDU) with individual outlet monitoring. This allows you to track the power consumption of each component in your system, ensuring that everything runs smoothly.

By paying attention to these aspects of power management, you can create a stable and efficient environment for training your machine learning models. This careful attention to power management will help maintain the longevity and effectiveness of your hardware, ensuring consistent and reliable performance.

2.7 Components of a Training System: Orchestrating the Hardware

Creating a comprehensive and effective training system for Large Language Models (LLMs) involves orchestrating various components to function

35

harmoniously. This integrated system brings together a diverse range of resources.

First, the hardware infrastructure forms the physical foundation of the training system. It includes powerful processing units such as Graphics Processing Units (GPUs) or specialized Tensor Processing Units (TPUs) designed for the massive parallel computations required for LLM training. Additionally, the hardware needs sufficient memory (RAM) to hold the model and data during training and high-bandwidth networking to efficiently transfer data between different parts of the system.

Next, software frameworks provide the tools and libraries necessary to implement the training process. Popular options include TensorFlow, PyTorch, and JAX, which offer functionalities like automatic differentiation, optimized tensor operations, and distributed training capabilities. These frameworks are essential for developing and managing the training workflows.

Sophisticated algorithms act as the "brains" of the training process. They dictate how the LLM learns from the data, incorporating optimization algorithms, regularization techniques, and architectural innovations to enhance model performance and accuracy.

High-quality training data serves as the fuel that powers the LLM. It consists of vast amounts of text and code, carefully curated and preprocessed to be suitable for training. The quality and diversity of the training data significantly impact the model's ability to generalize and perform well on various tasks.

These four elements are not isolated entities. The hardware must be compatible with the software framework to ensure efficient execution. The algorithms need to be designed to effectively utilize the hardware resources. The data must be preprocessed in a way that aligns with the algorithms and software framework. The overall effectiveness of the training system relies on the synergistic interaction of these components, ensuring that they work together

37

seamlessly to achieve optimal results. By understanding and optimizing each of these elements, you can create a powerful and efficient LLM training system.

2.8 The Role of Cloud Providers: Managing Resources Efficiently

Cloud providers are essential in managing computational resources, acting as coordinators for the allocation of GPUs and TPUs based on your model's requirements. They go beyond providing just hardware, offering managed services that support various stages of machine learning, from data storage to model training and deployment.

One of the managed services is Amazon SageMaker, a comprehensive machine learning platform that includes tools for data preparation, model training, and deployment. This platform streamlines the entire machine learning workflow, making it easier to develop and deploy models.

38

Another example is the Google AI Platform, which offers a range of services for building and deploying AI models. This includes Cloud AutoML and AI Platform Training, which provide powerful tools for creating and refining machine learning models.

Azure Machine Learning is another valuable cloud-based service. It provides a collaborative environment for building and deploying models, facilitating teamwork and enhancing productivity. This service supports various stages of the machine learning process, from data ingestion to model evaluation and deployment.

Using a managed service can simplify the process of training and deploying your large language models (LLMs). These services offer robust infrastructure and tools that make it easier to manage the complexities of machine learning projects, allowing you to focus more on developing and refining your models. By leveraging the capabilities of cloud providers, you can optimize resource allocation and enhance the efficiency of your machine learning tasks.

2.9 Efficient Resource Allocation: Maximizing Performance

Efficiently allocating resources is crucial for achieving optimal performance during the training of large language models (LLMs). The balancing act involves the strategic use of CPUs, GPUs, memory, and storage to ensure that your system performs at its best.

To start, using efficient data loaders is essential for feeding data to the GPUs as quickly as possible. This helps to minimize idle times and keeps the training process running smoothly. Experimenting with different batch sizes is another important step. Finding the right batch size can help you strike a balance between memory usage and training speed, ensuring that your system is neither underutilized nor overloaded.

If you can't fit a large enough batch size into memory, gradient accumulation can be a helpful technique. By accumulating gradients over several smaller batches, you can simulate the effect of having a larger batch size without exceeding your system's memory limits.

40

A practical tip for maximizing performance is to use profiling tools to identify bottlenecks in your training pipeline. These tools can help you pinpoint areas where your system is slowing down, allowing you to make targeted adjustments and improvements.

By focusing on efficient resource allocation, you can optimize the performance of your LLM training, ensuring that your system runs smoothly and effectively. This approach helps to maximize both the speed and accuracy of your training process, leading to better results and more efficient use of your computational resources.

2.10 Storage Management: Optimizing Data Access

Managing storage effectively is essential for maintaining peak performance during the training of machine learning models. One key aspect is data locality, which involves storing your data as close as possible to the compute resources. This proximity minimizes data transfer times and ensures that your system can access the data quickly and efficiently.

41

Another important step is data preprocessing. By preprocessing your data, you can reduce its size and complexity, making it easier to handle and process during training. This can involve cleaning the data, normalizing it, and performing any necessary transformations to prepare it for analysis.

Data compression is also a valuable technique. Using data compression techniques, you can reduce the amount of storage space required for your data. This not only saves space but also speeds up data transfer and loading times, further enhancing performance.

A practical tip is to use a distributed file system to store and access your data. Distributed file systems allow you to spread your data across multiple servers or storage devices, ensuring high availability and reliability. This setup can handle large datasets more efficiently, providing a scalable solution for your storage needs.

By implementing these strategies, you can optimize data access and ensure that your machine learning training system runs smoothly and efficiently. This knowledge will help you make informed decisions about storage management, ultimately improving the performance and productivity of your training processes.

2.11 Power and Cooling – The Often-Forgotten Essentials

Beyond the glamorous aspects of algorithms and vast datasets, the essential elements of power and cooling underpin the entire LLM training enterprise. These factors are often considered afterthoughts, but a failure in either can cripple a training run, leading to lost time, wasted resources, and delayed progress.

Power supply is the lifeblood of computation. Training large language models (LLMs) requires a massive and consistent supply of electrical power. Insufficient power can lead to system instability, causing components to malfunction, crashes, data corruption, and inconsistent training results. Performance throttling can occur when hardware automatically reduces its clock speed, significantly slowing down the training process.

43

Prolonged exposure to unstable power can shorten the lifespan of expensive hardware components.

A well-designed power infrastructure is crucial. This includes ensuring that power supply units (PSUs) can deliver the required wattage for all components at peak load, with a margin for safety and future expansion. Implementing measures to minimize voltage fluctuations ensures a clean, consistent power supply. Incorporating redundant power supplies provides backup power in case of a PSU failure.

Cooling is equally important. As GPUs and TPUs crunch through trillions of calculations, they generate immense amounts of heat. Without effective cooling, this heat can quickly lead to overheating, damaging sensitive electronic components and leading to permanent hardware failure. Overheating triggers thermal throttling, drastically reducing processing speeds. High operating temperatures accelerate the degradation of components, shortening their useful life.

44

An adequate cooling system can involve a combination of methods. Air cooling uses fans and heatsinks to dissipate heat directly from the components. Liquid cooling uses liquid coolants to absorb heat from the components and transport it away to a radiator. Immersion cooling involves immersing the entire server or components in a dielectric fluid that directly absorbs heat. Strategic airflow management is essential in designing the data center or server room to ensure proper airflow and prevent hotspots from forming.

In summary, a reliable power supply and an effective cooling system are not mere afterthoughts but critical components of a successful LLM training environment. These elements ensure the longevity and effectiveness of your hardware, allowing you to achieve optimal performance and productivity in your machine learning tasks.

2.12 The Importance of Reliable Power Supply

Having a stable power supply is crucial for maintaining consistent performance during the training of high-

45

performance computing systems. Without reliable power, your hardware could be vulnerable to disruptions that negatively impact the training process.

Clean power is essential to protect your hardware from power surges and brownouts. Using a surge protector or an uninterruptible power supply (UPS) can help safeguard your equipment from sudden voltage spikes or drops. These devices ensure that your system receives a steady flow of power, preventing potential damage and data loss.

Another important consideration is redundancy. By using a redundant power supply, you can ensure that your system remains operational even if one power supply fails. This backup mechanism provides an additional layer of reliability, minimizing the risk of downtime during critical training sessions.

To ensure that your electrical system can handle the power requirements of your training setup, it's advisable to consult with an electrician. They can assess your current infrastructure and recommend any

46

necessary upgrades or adjustments. This proactive approach helps to prevent power-related issues and ensures that your system runs smoothly.

By paying attention to these aspects of power supply management, you can create a more robust and reliable environment for training your high-performance computing systems. This attention to detail is essential for maintaining the longevity and effectiveness of your hardware.

2.13 The Role of Cooling in High-Performance Computing

Efficient cooling plays a crucial role in managing the heat generated during the training of high-performance computing systems. Without proper cooling, components can overheat, leading to reduced performance and potential hardware failure. Different cooling options are available, each with its advantages and considerations.

Air cooling is the most common and least expensive solution. It uses fans to circulate air and dissipate heat

47

from the components. While effective for many setups, it might not be sufficient for more demanding tasks that generate a lot of heat.

Liquid cooling offers a more efficient solution than air cooling. It uses a liquid coolant to absorb and transfer heat away from the components. Although it is more effective, liquid cooling systems are also more expensive and complex to install and maintain.

Immersion cooling is the most effective cooling solution available. It involves submerging the entire system in a non-conductive liquid that efficiently dissipates heat. While this method provides the best cooling performance, it is also the most expensive and complex to implement.

To ensure optimal cooling, it's important to maintain good airflow within your system. Proper airflow helps to dissipate heat more effectively, reducing the risk of overheating. Additionally, monitoring the temperature of your components is essential. By keeping an eye on

48

temperature levels, you can take action before any component overheats and causes damage.

For the best results, consider using a combination of cooling solutions. This approach allows you to balance cost, complexity, and cooling efficiency, ensuring that your high-performance computing system operates smoothly and reliably.

Understanding the role of cooling and the various options available will help you make informed decisions about how to best manage heat generation in your high-performance computing setup. This knowledge is essential for maintaining the longevity and performance of your hardware.

Example 1: Machine Translation Using GPUs

Imagine you're developing a machine translation model. By leveraging the parallel processing power of multiple GPUs, you can process large datasets efficiently, enabling faster training and more accurate translations.

49

For the hardware setup, you would use a cluster of servers, each equipped with 4-8 high-end NVIDIA GPUs, such as the A100 or H100. These GPUs provide the necessary computational power to handle large-scale machine translation tasks.

Your software stack would include PyTorch or TensorFlow, both of which are popular deep learning frameworks. Additionally, you would use distributed training libraries that allow the model to be trained across multiple GPUs, further speeding up the process.

As for the cloud provider, you could choose from AWS, GCP, or Azure. These platforms offer robust infrastructure and services to support large-scale machine learning tasks, making it easier to manage and scale your resources.

The main focus of this setup is to minimize training time while maximizing translation accuracy. By using multiple GPUs and distributed training, you can train your model more quickly and achieve more accurate translations, making it a powerful solution for machine translation tasks.

Example 2: Healthcare Image Recognition Using TPUs

In the healthcare sector, using image recognition models trained with Tensor Processing Units (TPUs) can greatly enhance the analysis of medical imaging, which is crucial for early diagnosis. TPUs, which are specialized hardware accelerators designed to expedite machine learning tasks, can process large volumes of medical images quickly and efficiently.

For setting up this system, you would utilize the Google Cloud Platform (GCP) and specifically make use of TPU Pods. These provide the necessary computational power to handle intensive image analysis tasks. The software stack for this setup includes TensorFlow, a highly popular deep learning framework developed by Google, which is well-suited for developing and training image recognition models.

51

By using GCP as your cloud provider, you can leverage their infrastructure to ensure that your setup is both scalable and capable of real-time image analysis. This means that your image recognition models can be deployed to analyze medical images swiftly, providing critical support for early diagnosis and treatment planning.

The main focus here is on achieving high speed and scalability to facilitate real-time analysis. This capability is particularly beneficial in medical settings, where timely and accurate image interpretation can significantly impact patient outcomes. Using TPUs and the cloud infrastructure provided by GCP, healthcare providers can implement advanced image recognition systems that enhance the efficiency and effectiveness of diagnostic processes.

Example 3: A Small Business Building a Custom Chatbot

Imagine a small business wants to develop a custom chatbot to manage customer service inquiries. They lack the resources to train a large language model (LLM) from scratch, but they can still create an effective solution by fine-tuning an existing pre-trained model on their specific customer service data.

To start, their hardware setup would involve a single server equipped with 2-4 mid-range NVIDIA GPUs, such as the RTX 3090 or RTX 4080. This setup provides the necessary computational power to handle the fine-tuning process efficiently. For the software stack, they would use Hugging Face Transformers and PyTorch, two powerful tools that simplify working with pre-trained models and deep learning frameworks.

They would likely use a Virtual Private Server (VPS) provider or a small cloud instance to host their server, offering a flexible and cost-effective solution for their needs.

The strategy involves fine-tuning an existing pre-trained LLM on the specific customer service data they have collected. This approach allows the chatbot to learn

53

from actual customer interactions, making it more adept at handling inquiries relevant to the business.

Understanding the components of a machine learning training system is vital for success. Each element, from hardware and software to data management and power supply, plays a critical role in creating an environment that supports innovation and productivity. This chapter provides a strong foundation for grasping these components and making informed decisions about LLM training infrastructure.

The following chapters will build upon this foundation, diving deeper into software, data preparation, and training techniques to enhance your understanding and capabilities in developing effective machine learning systems. This knowledge equips you with the tools to create a custom chatbot tailored to your business's unique needs, even with limited resources.

Machine   Healthcare   Small Businesss

CHAPTER 3: The Software Infrastructure Behind Large Language Models (LLMs)

Pulling Back the Curtain on LLM Software

Welcome back to our journey through the world of large language models (LLMs)! By now, you've got a sense of what LLMs are (Chapter 1) and how they're shaping our digital lives (Chapter 2). But have you ever wondered what's happening behind the scenes to make these incredible tools work? That's what this chapter is all about—pulling back the curtain on the software infrastructure that powers LLMs.

Think of software infrastructure as the foundation of a house. You don't see it every day, but without it, the walls wouldn't stand, and the roof wouldn't stay up. For LLMs, this foundation includes the tools, frameworks, and processes that help developers train these models to understand and generate human-like language. Whether it's a chatbot answering your questions or a tool translating a foreign language, none of it would be

56

possible without the clever software systems we're about to explore.

In this chapter, we'll break it down into bite-sized pieces. We'll look at the frameworks that build LLMs, the pre-trained models that give them a head start, the step-by-step workflow to bring them to life, and how developers scale things up when the going gets tough. Don't worry if terms like "GPU" or "distributed training" sound intimidating—we'll keep it simple, with examples and tips you can wrap your head around. Ready? Let's get started!

3.1 Frameworks: Tools for Building LLMs (The Baker's Oven)

Imagine you're baking a cake. You need the right ingredients (like flour and sugar) and tools (like a mixer and oven) to make it delicious. For LLMs, the "ingredients" are data and algorithms, and the "tools" are software frameworks—special programs that make building and training these models easier and faster. Let's meet some of the key players.

57

3.2 PyTorch: The Pythonic Powerhouse

PyTorch has become a leading framework in the research and development of large language models (LLMs), thanks to its flexibility, ease of use, and strong community support. Think of it as having a versatile and well-equipped kitchen.

One of PyTorch's standout features is its dynamic computation graphs, which allow for more flexible and intuitive model development. This means you can change the model's structure on the fly, making it easier to experiment and innovate. PyTorch is designed with a Python-first approach, ensuring seamless integration with the Python ecosystem. This makes it accessible and familiar to anyone comfortable with Python.

Another major advantage of PyTorch is its strong support for NVIDIA GPUs, including CUDA and cuDNN. This means you can leverage powerful hardware to accelerate your computations, making training large models more feasible. PyTorch also boasts a large and

58

active community, providing a wealth of tutorials, libraries, and pre-trained models that you can utilize to get started quickly and troubleshoot any issues you encounter.

Several popular libraries work seamlessly with PyTorch. The Transformers library from Hugging Face is essential for working with pre-trained LLMs, providing tools and models for a wide range of NLP tasks. PyTorch Lightning simplifies the training process with a high-level API, making it easier to write clean and maintainable code. torchtext offers tools for data loading and preprocessing, helping you prepare your text data for analysis or model training.

If you're comfortable with Python and looking for a flexible, well-supported framework, PyTorch is an excellent choice. Its features and community support make it a powerful tool for developing and training large language models, ensuring that your projects are both innovative and efficient.

3.3 TensorFlow: Google's Production-Ready Framework

TensorFlow is a well-known deep learning framework developed by Google. It's highly regarded for its scalability, production readiness, and robust ecosystem, making it similar to an industrial-grade baking factory in its efficiency.

One of its key features is the use of static computation graphs, which are optimized for performance and deployment. This means that TensorFlow can handle complex computations efficiently. TensorBoard is another powerful feature, providing a visualization tool that allows you to monitor the training progress of your models, giving you insights into how well they are performing.

TensorFlow also includes the Keras API, a high-level interface that simplifies the process of building and training models. This makes it accessible even for those who may not be experts in deep learning. Additionally, TensorFlow has excellent support for Google's Tensor

60

Processing Units (TPUs), specialized hardware designed to accelerate machine learning tasks.

Several popular libraries work seamlessly with TensorFlow. The Transformers library from Hugging Face is compatible with TensorFlow, allowing you to leverage pre-trained models for various NLP tasks. TensorFlow Datasets provides access to a wide range of pre-built datasets, making it easier to train your models with diverse data. TF Agents is a library specifically designed for reinforcement learning, providing tools and algorithms to help you develop and train reinforcement learning models.

If you are aiming for production deployment and want to take advantage of Google's infrastructure, TensorFlow is an excellent choice. Its comprehensive features and strong ecosystem make it a powerful tool for deep learning applications, ensuring that your models are both performant and scalable.

3.4 JAX: The New Kid on the Block

JAX is a relatively new framework that is quickly gaining popularity in the large language model (LLM) community because of its impressive performance and flexibility. Think of it as the latest, innovative kitchen gadget that everyone is excited about.

One of JAX's standout features is automatic differentiation, which makes it easy to compute gradients needed for training. This significantly simplifies the process of optimizing models. Another key feature is just-in-time (JIT) compilation, which optimizes your code for better performance, making it run faster and more efficiently. JAX also supports both NVIDIA GPUs and Google TPUs, giving you the flexibility to run your computations on powerful hardware. Additionally, JAX encourages a functional programming style, which promotes writing clean and maintainable code.

There are also some popular libraries associated with JAX. Haiku is a neural network library specifically

62

designed for JAX, offering tools to build and train neural networks. Another library, Flax, focuses on scalability and provides additional features for building complex models.

For those interested in cutting-edge research and looking to leverage the performance advantages of JAX, it's worth exploring this powerful framework. It offers a modern and efficient approach to building and training large language models, making it a valuable tool for anyone in the field.

3.5 Pre-trained Models: Where to Start (Standing on the Shoulders of Giants)

Training an LLM from scratch is like teaching a baby every word in the dictionary—it takes a lot of time and effort. Luckily, developers don't always start from zero. They use pre-trained models, which are LLMs that have already been taught the basics on giant datasets, like books, websites, and more. These models are ready to be fine-tuned—tweaked for specific tasks like writing emails or analyzing movie reviews.

63

3.6 The Hugging Face Hub: A Treasure Trove of Pre-trained Models

The Hugging Face Hub is a central repository that offers a wealth of pre-trained models, datasets, and evaluation metrics. This platform provides a convenient way to discover and utilize pre-trained models for a wide range of natural language processing (NLP) tasks.

One of the standout features of the Hugging Face Hub is its extensive collection of thousands of pre-trained models. These models cover a wide array of languages and tasks, making it easier for users to find a model that fits their specific needs.

The platform also offers an easy model loading system. With a simple API, users can load and use pre-trained models in PyTorch and TensorFlow, streamlining the integration process. Each model on the Hugging Face Hub comes with detailed model cards, which provide comprehensive information about the model, including its architecture, training data, and performance metrics.

The Hugging Face Hub is supported by a vibrant community of researchers and developers who contribute models and datasets. This collaborative environment fosters innovation and ensures that the repository remains up-to-date with the latest advancements in NLP.

For those embarking on an LLM project, a practical tip is to start by exploring the Hugging Face Hub. This treasure trove of pre-trained models can help you find a suitable starting point for your specific task, saving time and resources in the initial stages of your project.

3.7 Popular Pre-trained Models

There are several well-known pre-trained models in the field of natural language processing (NLP) that have gained popularity for their impressive capabilities and applications.

One famous pre-trained model is BERT, which stands for Bidirectional Encoder Representations from Transformers. BERT is excellent at understanding context in sentences because it analyzes words from

65

both directions, left-to-right and right-to-left. It has been trained on vast amounts of text, so it already possesses extensive knowledge about language. This makes BERT particularly suitable for tasks that require natural language understanding.

GPT, or Generative Pre-trained Transformer, is another powerful model. It excels in text generation tasks, enabling it to create coherent and contextually relevant text based on given prompts. GPT's versatility and ability to generate human-like text have made it a popular choice for various applications.

T5, which stands for Text-to-Text Transfer Transformer, is a versatile model designed for a wide range of NLP tasks. It treats every NLP problem as a text-to-text problem, making it highly adaptable and effective in handling different types of text-based tasks.

RoBERTa, or Robustly Optimized BERT Approach, is an improved version of BERT. It achieves state-of-the-art results on many NLP benchmarks by enhancing the

66

training process and making the model more robust and efficient.

Llama 2 is a family of open-source large language models released by Meta. These models are designed for both research and commercial use, offering a range of capabilities and applications for various NLP tasks.

Understanding these popular pre-trained models can provide a solid foundation for exploring and leveraging their capabilities in different NLP projects. Each model brings unique strengths, making them valuable tools for various language-related tasks.

3.8 Key Steps in Data Preprocessing

Data preprocessing involves a series of steps designed to clean, transform, and prepare the data for training large language models (LLMs). These steps may include:

Data cleaning is the initial step, where irrelevant information is removed. This might involve stripping HTML tags from web pages, deleting unnecessary columns from a dataset, or filtering out noise from

67

audio recordings. Handling missing values is another crucial part, which can be done by imputing missing data with estimated values or removing rows with missing entries. Correcting errors such as typos, inconsistent date formats, or contradictory information is also essential to ensure the data's accuracy.

Tokenization is the process of breaking down text into smaller units called tokens, which can be words, subwords, or characters. It is a fundamental step in preparing text for machine learning models. There are different methods of tokenization, each with its strengths and weaknesses. For instance, Byte Pair Encoding (BPE) is commonly used in LLMs to handle out-of-vocabulary words effectively.

Normalization involves converting text into a consistent format, such as changing all characters to lowercase. This helps the model generalize better by treating "The" and "the" as the same word. Techniques like stemming and lemmatization reduce words to their root form. For example, words like "running," "ran," and "runs" might be reduced to "run." Removing stop words, which are

68

common words like "the," "a," and "is" that often don't carry much meaning, can reduce the size of the data and improve training efficiency.

Data augmentation involves creating new training examples from existing ones by applying various transformations. For example, translating a sentence into another language and then back into the original language can create a slightly different version of the same sentence. This technique helps the model generalize better and become more robust to variations in the data.

Data balancing addresses the issue of imbalanced datasets, where some classes are much more common than others, leading to biased models. Techniques such as oversampling the minority classes or undersampling the majority classes can help to create a more balanced dataset.

Neglecting preprocessing can have significant consequences. It may lead to poor model performance, biased results, and an inability to generalize well to new

69

data. Therefore, investing time in data preprocessing is crucial for building effective and robust language models.

Code Example (PyTorch):

```
from transformers import BertTokenizer, BertForSequenceClassification
from torch.utils.data import Dataset, DataLoader
import torch

# Load the pre-trained BERT model and tokenizer
tokenizer = BertTokenizer.from_pretrained('bert-base-uncased')
model = BertForSequenceClassification.from_pretrained('bert-base-uncased', num_labels=3)

# Define a custom dataset class
class IMDBDataset(Dataset):
    def __init__(self, encodings, labels):
        self.encodings = encodings
        self.labels = labels

    def __getitem__(self, idx):
        item = {key: torch.tensor(val[idx]) for key, val in self.encodings.items()}
        item['labels'] = torch.tensor(self.labels[idx])
        return item

    def __len__(self):
        return len(self.labels)
```

continued on next page...

70

```
# load and tokenize the data (replace with your actual dataset loading)
train_texts = ["This movie is great!", "I hated this film."]
train_labels = [1, 0]  # 1 for positive, 0 for negative
encodings = tokenizer(train_texts, truncation=True, padding=True)

# Create the dataset and dataloader
train_dataset = IMDBDataset(encodings, train_labels)
train_loader = DataLoader(train_dataset, batch_size=16, shuffle=True)

# Training loop (simplified)
optimizer = torch.optim.AdamW(model.parameters(), lr=5e-5)
model.train()
for batch in train_loader:
    optimizer.zero_grad()
    input_ids = batch['input_ids']
    attention_mask = batch['attention_mask']
    labels = batch['labels']
    outputs = model(input_ids, attention_mask=attention_mask, labels=labels)
    loss = outputs.loss
    loss.backward()
    optimizer.step()
```

Practical Tip: Use Hugging Face

Want to try this yourself? Check out Hugging Face, a website with tons of pre-trained models like BERT, plus easy-to-use tools. You can download a model, fine-tune it with a small dataset (even a few hundred sentences), and see it work—all without being a coding genius. It's a beginner's dream!

71

3.9 Data Preprocessing: Preparing the Fuel for the LLM Engine (Cleaning and Refining the Ingredients)

The Critical Role of Data in LLM Training

Large Language Models (LLMs) possess an impressive capacity to generate human-like text, translate languages, and answer questions with remarkable fluency. However, the capabilities of an LLM are inextricably linked to the quality and nature of the data it is trained on. Simply put, LLMs are only as good as the data they are trained on. This underscores the critical importance of meticulous data management throughout the LLM development lifecycle.

The Crucial Role of Data Preprocessing

Raw data, in its natural state, is often messy, inconsistent, and riddled with noise. It can contain errors, biases, irrelevant information, and formatting inconsistencies that, if left unaddressed, can significantly degrade the performance of the LLM. This is where data preprocessing comes in. Effective data preprocessing is essential for ensuring that your LLM

72

learns accurate and relevant patterns. It's the process of transforming raw, unstructured data into a clean, consistent, and readily usable format that is suitable for training the model.

The Analogy: Cooking Preparation

Consider the analogy of preparing a gourmet meal. It's like cleaning and chopping the vegetables before you start cooking. You wouldn't throw unwashed, unchopped vegetables directly into a pot and expect a delicious result. Similarly, you cannot simply feed raw data to an LLM and expect it to learn effectively. Just as a chef meticulously prepares their ingredients, a data scientist must carefully preprocess the data to ensure the best possible outcome.

Key Steps in Data Preprocessing

Data preprocessing involves a series of steps designed to clean, transform, and prepare the data for training large language models (LLMs). These steps may include:

3.10 Data Cleaning: Removing Noise and Inconsistencies

The initial and often most critical step in data preprocessing is **Data Cleaning**. Raw text data, especially when sourced from diverse origins like the web, is frequently messy and contains elements that are irrelevant, incorrect, or inconsistent. Cleaning aims to remove this "noise" to ensure the data fed into the LLM is as accurate and meaningful as possible, directly impacting the model's learning quality.

Key data cleaning tasks often include:

- **Removing Irrelevant Content:** This involves stripping out elements that don't contribute to the linguistic understanding needed by the model. Common examples include:

  - **HTML/XML Tags:** Removing markup from web-scraped text (e.g., <p>, <div>).

  - **Special Characters/Emojis (Task Dependent):** Removing characters that might not be relevant to the specific task,

74

though sometimes emojis carry sentiment and should be kept or replaced.

- **Boilerplate Text:** Removing standard headers, footers, navigation menus, or advertisements from web pages.

- **Handling Formatting Issues:** Correcting inconsistent whitespace (extra spaces, tabs, line breaks) to standardize text structure.

- **Correcting Errors:** Addressing obvious inaccuracies where possible:

  - **Typos and Spelling Mistakes:** Using spell-checking libraries or techniques to correct common errors.

  - **Inconsistent Formatting:** Standardizing things like date formats, capitalization (often handled in Normalization), or numerical representations.

- **(Optional) Handling Missing or Incomplete Data:** While less common for raw text corpus

75

building, if working with structured text data (like datasets with specific fields), deciding how to handle missing entries (e.g., removing the record, imputing a placeholder) might be necessary.

Effective data cleaning prevents the LLM from learning incorrect patterns, reduces noise that can hinder performance, and ultimately leads to a more reliable and accurate model. It's often an iterative process, requiring careful examination of the raw data to identify and address specific types of noise effectively.

3.11 Tokenization: Breaking Down Language into Processable Units

Before a Large Language Model can "understand" or process human language, the continuous stream of text needs to be segmented into smaller, discrete pieces. This fundamental preparation step is called **Tokenization**, where text is broken down into units known as **tokens**.

Depending on the chosen tokenization strategy, these tokens might be:

76

- **Words:** The most intuitive approach, splitting text based on spaces and punctuation (e.g., "Large", "Language", "Models").

- **Subwords:** Breaking words into smaller, meaningful parts (e.g., "tokenization" might become "token" + "ization"). This is very common in modern LLMs.

- **Characters:** Splitting text into individual letters, numbers, and symbols (e.g., "L", "L", "M").

Models operate on these tokens rather than raw sentences, making tokenization essential for input processing and output generation. While various methods exist, subword tokenization techniques like **Byte Pair Encoding (BPE)**, WordPiece, or SentencePiece are widely used in LLMs. These methods are particularly effective because they can handle vast vocabularies, rare words, and even words not seen during training (out-of-vocabulary words) by breaking them down into known subword units, rather than treating them as completely unknown symbols. The

77

choice of tokenizer significantly impacts how the model perceives and processes language.

3.12 Normalization: Standardizing Text for Consistency

Once text is tokenized, **normalization** techniques are often applied to convert words into a more consistent format. This process reduces superficial variations in text that don't typically alter core meaning, helping the model generalize better and treat similar concepts uniformly. Key normalization steps include:

- **Case Folding:** This commonly involves converting all text to a single case, usually **lowercase**. Doing so ensures the model doesn't treat words like "Model" and "model" as distinct entities simply due to capitalization, promoting consistent interpretation.

- **Stemming and Lemmatization:** These techniques aim to reduce words to their base or root form.

78

- **Stemming:** A simpler, rule-based process that typically chops off word endings (prefixes/suffixes) to get to a common stem (e.g., "running," "ran," "runs" might all become "run"; "studies," "studying" might become "studi"). It's fast but can sometimes result in non-dictionary words or conflate different meanings.

- **Lemmatization:** A more sophisticated approach that uses vocabulary analysis and morphological understanding to return the actual dictionary form of a word (the lemma) (e.g., "running," "ran," "runs" become "run"; "studies," "studying" become "study"; "better" becomes "good"). Lemmatization is generally more accurate but computationally more intensive than stemming.

  Both techniques help the model recognize different grammatical forms of the same

79

core word as being related, reducing the vocabulary size it needs to manage.

- **Stop Word Removal:** This involves identifying and removing extremely common words (e.g., "the," "a," "is," "in," "on," "and") that often contribute little unique semantic meaning for certain tasks. Removing stop words can significantly reduce the size of the data, potentially improving training efficiency and helping the model focus on more content-rich terms. However, whether to remove stop words is highly dependent on the specific task; for tasks requiring understanding of syntax, nuance, or full sentence structure, removing them can be detrimental.

Choosing which normalization steps to apply depends heavily on the specific LLM task and the characteristics of the dataset. Libraries like NLTK or SpaCy in Python provide tools for implementing these techniques effectively.

80

3.13 Data Augmentation: Enhancing Dataset Diversity

Beyond cleaning and structuring, **data augmentation** is a powerful strategy for increasing the size and diversity of your training dataset, especially when source data is limited or lacks variety. The core idea is to create new, synthetic training examples by applying controlled transformations to your existing data.

This technique significantly improves a model's ability to **generalize** to unseen inputs and increases its **robustness** against minor variations in language, much like exposing a student to different explanations of the same concept improves their understanding. Effectively, augmentation teaches the LLM that different phrasings can carry similar meanings.

Several common text augmentation techniques include:

- **Synonym Replacement:** Swapping specific words with their appropriate synonyms (e.g., replacing 'content' with 'happy', 'fast' with 'quick') introduces semantic variety without changing the core message.

81

- **Random Insertion/Deletion:** Adding random, often common, words (like articles or prepositions) into sentences or removing non-critical words forces the model to become less reliant on exact sentence structure and focus more on core context.

- **Back-Translation:** Translating text into another language and then translating it back to the original (e.g., English -> Spanish -> English) often yields paraphrased versions with slightly different grammatical structures or vocabulary while preserving the essential meaning.

- **Text Paraphrasing:** Utilizing specialized tools or models designed to rephrase sentences or passages while maintaining the original intent.

When implementing augmentation, it's crucial to apply transformations carefully to ensure they **do not fundamentally alter the original meaning or the associated label** (if doing supervised learning). Over-aggressive augmentation can introduce noise and confuse the model rather than strengthening it.

82

Consider leveraging established libraries (like nlpaug or functions within frameworks like Hugging Face's datasets) that offer controlled augmentation methods. It's also wise to perform quality checks on a sample of the augmented data to ensure its validity and continued relevance to your specific task. Investing time in thoughtful data augmentation can significantly improve the performance and real-world adaptability of your LLM.

3.14 Data balancing

Data Balancing: Addressing Skewed Representations

While large-scale pre-training often relies on massive, diverse corpora, **Data Balancing** becomes a critical consideration, particularly when fine-tuning LLMs for specific *supervised learning tasks* such as text classification, sentiment analysis, or intent recognition. This addresses the common issue of **imbalanced datasets**, where certain categories or classes are significantly overrepresented compared to others.

83

The Problem with Imbalance:

If a dataset is heavily skewed (e.g., 95% positive reviews and 5% negative reviews), a model trained on it will likely become biased towards the majority class. It can achieve high overall accuracy simply by predicting the dominant category most of the time, while performing very poorly on the underrepresented minority class(es). This leads to models that are not truly useful or fair in real-world scenarios where minority cases might be important (e.g., detecting rare diseases, identifying specific types of toxic comments).

Common Balancing Techniques:

Several techniques can be employed *before* or *during* training to mitigate the effects of imbalance:

1. **Oversampling:**

   - **What it is:** Increasing the number of instances in the minority class(es). The simplest method is randomly duplicating existing minority samples.

84

- **Effect:** Provides the model with more exposure to the minority class.

- **Risk:** Simple duplication can lead to the model overfitting on the specific minority examples it has seen repeatedly.

2. **Undersampling:**

- **What it is:** Decreasing the number of instances in the majority class(es). The simplest method is randomly removing majority samples.

- **Effect:** Prevents the majority class from dominating the learning process.

- **Risk:** May discard potentially valuable information contained within the removed majority class data, especially if the dataset is not very large to begin with.

3. **Synthetic Data Generation (e.g., SMOTE):**

- **What it is:** Creating *new*, artificial data points for the minority class(es). Techniques like **SMOTE (Synthetic**

85

Minority Over-sampling Technique) generate synthetic samples by interpolating between existing minority class instances in the feature space.

- **Effect:** Increases minority representation without simple duplication, often leading to better model generalization than basic oversampling.

- **Consideration:** Requires careful implementation, especially with high-dimensional text data.

4. **Cost-Sensitive Learning:**

- **What it is:** Modifying the model's learning algorithm (rather than the data itself) to assign a higher misclassification cost to errors made on the minority class.

- **Effect:** Forces the model to pay more attention to correctly classifying the less frequent categories.

86

The choice of balancing technique depends on the dataset size, the degree of imbalance, and the specific task. Applying appropriate balancing strategies is crucial for developing LLMs that are not only accurate overall but also fair and effective across all relevant categories.

3.15 Neglecting

Preprocessing can have significant consequences. It may lead to poor model performance, biased results, and an inability to generalize well to new data. Therefore, investing time in data preprocessing is crucial for building effective and robust language models.

3.16 The Consequences of Neglecting Preprocessing

Neglecting to adequately preprocess data can have serious consequences for the performance of Large Language Models (LLMs). Noisy or inconsistent data can lead to reduced accuracy, causing the model to learn incorrect patterns and resulting in lower overall performance. If the data contains biases, the model will

87

likely perpetuate those biases. For example, a language model trained on a dataset that disproportionately portrays certain demographics in specific roles may learn to associate those demographics with those roles, leading to biased outputs.

Additionally, a model trained on poorly preprocessed data may struggle with generalization, meaning it won't perform well on new, unseen data. Dirty data can also make the training process slower and more difficult, increasing training time and resource consumption.

Data preprocessing is not a mere afterthought; it is a foundational step in developing effective LLMs. By investing the time and effort required to clean, transform, and prepare the data, you ensure that your LLM learns accurate and relevant patterns. This results in a more reliable, accurate, and unbiased model. Ultimately, the quality of your LLM reflects the quality of the data it is trained on, and data preprocessing is the key to unlocking the full potential of that data.

3.17 Key Data Preprocessing Steps

Data preprocessing is a crucial step in preparing your text data for analysis and training. It involves several important steps to ensure that your data is clean, consistent, and ready for use.

First, cleaning the data is essential. This involves removing irrelevant characters, HTML tags, and other noise from the text. This step helps to focus on the meaningful content.

Next is tokenization, where the text is split into tokens. Tokens are the basic units that the language model processes, such as words or subwords. This step makes it easier for the model to understand and analyze the text.

Vocabulary building follows tokenization. In this step, you create a vocabulary of all the unique tokens in your dataset. This helps the model understand the range of words it will encounter during training.

89

Normalization is another important step. It involves converting the text into a consistent format, such as converting all characters to lowercase or uppercase. This ensures uniformity and reduces variability in the text.

Stemming and lemmatization are techniques used to reduce words to their root form. For example, words like "running" and "ran" would be reduced to "run." This helps the model recognize and process different forms of the same word.

Finally, stop word removal involves removing common words that do not carry much meaning, such as "the," "a," and "is." This step reduces noise and helps the model focus on more informative words.

3.18 Handling Large Datasets

When working with large datasets, it's crucial to use strategies that help manage memory and processing power efficiently. One useful technique is data streaming, which involves loading data in smaller, manageable batches rather than all at once. This

90

approach prevents running out of memory and ensures that the system remains responsive.

Another effective method is distributed data processing. Tools like Apache Spark allow you to process data in parallel across multiple machines. This significantly speeds up the processing time and enables handling larger datasets that a single machine might struggle with.

Memory mapping is another powerful technique. It involves loading data into memory-mapped files, allowing the system to access and manipulate large files quickly without consuming excessive memory. This method is particularly useful when working with large binary files or databases.

By employing these techniques, you can handle large datasets more efficiently, ensuring your system runs smoothly and your data processing tasks are completed effectively. Investing time in learning and applying these strategies will greatly benefit your work with large-scale data.

Example: Tokenization with Hugging Face tokenizers

```
from transformers import BertTokenizer

tokenizer = BertTokenizer.from_pretrained('bert-base-uncased')
text = "This is an example sentence."
tokens = tokenizer.tokenize(text)
print(tokens)
# Output: ['this', 'is', 'an', 'example', 'sentence', '.']
```

3.19 Data Augmentation

Data augmentation is all about increasing the size and diversity of your training dataset by creating new data points from existing ones. This is crucial for improving the performance and robustness of your language models (LLMs).

One common technique is synonym replacement, where you replace words in your text with their synonyms. This helps create variations of sentences, making the model more versatile. Another technique is random insertion, where you randomly insert words into your text. This adds variety and can help the model learn to handle different sentence structures. Random

92

deletion involves deleting random words from your text, which forces the model to understand and predict missing information. Back translation is another effective method where you translate the text into another language and then back to the original language. This often results in new sentence structures and vocabulary, enriching your dataset.

A practical tip is to invest time in data preprocessing. This effort can significantly improve the performance and robustness of your LLM, making it more adaptable and effective in real-world applications. By applying these data augmentation techniques, you'll create a richer and more diverse dataset, ultimately leading to a better-performing model.

3.20 The Workflow: From Idea to Deployment (The LLM Recipe)

Building a Large Language Model (LLM) isn't magic—it's a process with clear steps. Think of it like planning a road trip: you pick your car, map the route, drive, and then check if you arrived where you wanted. Here's how it works for LLMs.

93

First, you need to choose your tools. If speed is essential, grab a framework like PyTorch or TensorFlow, which are popular software options for AI. If you want a head start, pick a pre-trained model like BERT. Match your choices to your goal, whether it's translating Spanish to English or summarizing news articles.

Next, if you're starting with a pre-trained model, this step is about fine-tuning it. For example, if you're building a translator, you might fine-tune the model on Spanish-English sentence pairs. You can do this on your computer, but for bigger jobs, cloud services like Amazon Web Services (AWS) or Google Cloud offer extra power.

Then, set up your training environment. This is where GPUs like the NVIDIA A100 shine—they process data quickly. Using PyTorch or TensorFlow, you feed the model your data and let it learn. Picture it like training a dog: the more examples it sees, the better it gets at its task, like translating or summarizing.

94

Finally, test your model to see if it performs correctly. Does it translate "Hola" to "Hello" accurately? If it's good enough, deploy it—put it online, into an app, or wherever it's needed. Tools like AWS SageMaker can help host it so others can use it too.

Before going big, try a mini version first. Train on a tiny dataset, like 50 sentences, and see how it performs. It's quicker and helps you spot mistakes early, like realizing your translator thinks "cat" is "dog"!

By following these steps, you can build an effective LLM tailored to your specific needs.

3.21 Scaling with Distributed Training (The Puzzle Party)

Sometimes, an LLM needs to learn from billions of words—way too much for one computer to handle alone. That's where distributed training comes in. It's like splitting a huge puzzle among friends: everyone works on a piece, and together, you finish faster.

Distributed Training Strategies

Distributed training strategies are essential for efficiently training large language models (LLMs) by leveraging multiple machines to share the workload.

95

These strategies ensure that the training process is scalable and can handle large datasets and complex models effectively.

3.22 Data Parallelism: Scaling Out by Dividing the Data

Data Parallelism is the most common and often the simplest strategy for scaling LLM training across multiple devices (GPUs or TPUs). The core idea is to accelerate training by processing different parts of the data simultaneously.

Think of it like assigning chapters of a large book to several students to read and summarize concurrently. Each student reads their assigned chapter (data subset) using the same set of instructions (the model).

How it Works:

1. **Model Replication:** A complete copy of the Large Language Model is loaded onto the memory of each participating device (e.g., each GPU in a multi-GPU server).

96

2. **Data Batch Splitting:** The overall training data batch for a given step is divided into smaller mini-batches.

3. **Parallel Processing:** Each device processes its assigned mini-batch independently and in parallel. This involves:

   - Performing a **forward pass** through the model replica with the mini-batch data to get predictions.

   - Calculating the **loss** based on these predictions.

   - Performing a **backward pass** (backpropagation) to compute the **gradients** (the updates needed for the model's parameters) based on the loss from its specific mini-batch.

4. **Gradient Synchronization:** This is the crucial communication step. The gradients calculated independently on each device are collected,

97

typically aggregated (e.g., averaged or summed) across all devices. This yields a single, combined gradient update that reflects the learning from the entire original data batch.

5. **Parameter Update:** The aggregated gradient is then used to update the model parameters. This update is applied consistently across all model replicas on each device, ensuring they remain synchronized for the next training step.

Benefits:

- **Increased Throughput & Reduced Training Time:** By processing data chunks in parallel, the overall time required to train on large datasets is significantly reduced.

- **Larger Effective Batch Size:** It allows the model to effectively learn from a larger batch of data in each step (the sum of all mini-batches), which can lead to more stable gradient estimates and potentially faster convergence.

98

- **Simpler Implementation (Relatively):**
  Compared to model parallelism, data parallelism
  is often easier to implement using standard deep
  learning frameworks (like PyTorch's
  DistributedDataParallel or TensorFlow's
  MirroredStrategy).

Considerations:

- **Model Must Fit:** The entire model must fit into
  the memory of each individual device.

- **Communication Overhead:** The gradient
  synchronization step requires communication
  between devices, which can become a
  bottleneck, especially with many devices or slow
  interconnects.

In essence, data parallelism tackles scale by distributing
the data workload, allowing multiple copies of the
model to learn concurrently and then consolidating
their findings to update the shared understanding.

3.23 Model Parallelism: Dividing the Model Itself

When Large Language Models become truly massive—containing hundreds of billions or even trillions of parameters—they often exceed the memory capacity of even the largest single accelerator (GPU or TPU). In such scenarios, **Model Parallelism** becomes a necessity. Unlike data parallelism, which replicates the entire model on each device, model parallelism involves **splitting the model's architecture** across multiple devices.

Think of it like trying to assemble an enormous, intricate machine that's too large for one workbench. You'd distribute different sections or components of the machine across several adjacent workbenches, with workers passing parts between stations as needed.

100

How it Works (Common Approaches):

1. Pipeline Parallelism (Inter-Layer Parallelism):

- **Concept:** This is the most intuitive form. The model's layers are divided sequentially across devices. Device A might handle layers 1-10, Device B handles layers 11-20, Device C handles layers 21-30, and so on.

- **Data Flow:** A batch of data enters Device A, is processed through its assigned layers, the output (activations) is passed to Device B, processed through its layers, passed to Device C, and so forth. The process reverses for the backward pass (gradient calculation).

- **Analogy:** It operates like an **assembly line**. Each device is a station responsible for specific steps before passing the work-in-progress to the next station.

101

- **Challenge:** Can lead to "pipeline bubbles," where devices sit idle waiting for the previous stage to complete. Techniques like **micro-batching** (splitting the data batch into even smaller chunks that flow through the pipeline continuously) are used to mitigate this and keep devices utilized.

2. **Tensor Parallelism (Intra-Layer Parallelism):**

- **Concept:** Instead of splitting between layers, this approach splits the computations within a single large layer (like massive matrix multiplications in transformer blocks) across multiple devices. Each device computes part of the operation, and the results are combined via communication.

- **Use Case:** Particularly effective for very large embedding tables or transformer

102

layers that wouldn't fit on one device even by themselves.

- **Complexity:** Often more complex to implement than pipeline parallelism, requiring careful management of tensor slicing and communication patterns (e.g., using collective communication operations like all-gather or reduce-scatter).

- **Synergy:** Often used in conjunction with pipeline and/or data parallelism for extremely large models.

Why Use Model Parallelism?

- **Overcoming Memory Limits:** Its primary purpose is to enable the training of models that are simply too large for a single device's memory (VRAM).

- **Handling Massive Layers:** Tensor parallelism specifically addresses layers or components that are individually too large.

103

Challenges & Considerations:

- **Implementation Complexity:** Generally more complex to implement correctly than data parallelism, requiring careful partitioning of the model and managing inter-device dependencies.

- **Communication Overhead:** Significant amounts of data (activations during the forward pass, gradients during the backward pass) must be transferred between devices in the pipeline or within tensor splits. This inter-device communication can become a major performance bottleneck if not optimized.

- **Load Balancing:** Ensuring that the computational load is balanced reasonably across the devices involved in the split is crucial to avoid some devices sitting idle while others are overworked.

- **Framework Support:** Requires frameworks and libraries designed to handle model partitioning and inter-device communication efficiently (e.g.,

104

DeepSpeed, Megatron-LM, PyTorch's FSDP with certain configurations).

In summary, model parallelism is a critical scaling strategy employed when models outgrow single devices. It partitions the model itself across accelerators, enabling the training of exceptionally large LLMs, albeit typically with increased implementation complexity and communication overhead compared to data parallelism.

3.24 Pipeline Parallelism: The Model Assembly Line

Pipeline Parallelism is a specific and widely used form of **Model Parallelism**, designed to train models that are too large to fit onto a single device by distributing the computational workload sequentially across multiple accelerators (GPUs/TPUs). As the name suggests, it functions much like a factory **assembly line**.

How it Works:

1. **Model Staging:** The layers of the LLM are partitioned into sequential groups, called **stages**. Each stage (containing one or more layers) is assigned to a specific device. For instance, Device 1 might handle the initial embedding layers and early transformer blocks, Device 2 the middle blocks, and Device 3 the final blocks and output layer.

2. **Forward Pass Flow:** Input data (a mini-batch) enters the pipeline at the first device (Stage 1). After being processed through the layers in that

106

stage, the resulting intermediate activations are passed to the next device (Stage 2). This device performs its computations and passes its output activations onward. This continues until the data reaches the final stage and the final output (e.g., predictions) is produced.

3. **Backward Pass Flow:** The process reverses for the backward pass (gradient calculation). The loss is calculated based on the final output, and gradients are computed on the last device. These gradients are then passed backward through the pipeline, stage by stage, allowing each device to calculate the gradients for its specific layers based on the gradients received from the subsequent stage.

4. **Micro-Batching for Efficiency:** A naive implementation of this pipeline would lead to significant idle time, as devices early in the pipeline finish their forward pass and wait for the entire batch to complete before starting the backward pass (and vice-versa). This inefficiency

107

is known as the "pipeline bubble." To mitigate this, modern pipeline parallelism heavily relies on **micro-batching**. The main data batch is split into smaller micro-batches. As soon as the first stage finishes processing the first micro-batch, it passes the result to the second stage and immediately starts processing the second micro-batch. This interleaving of computation across different micro-batches keeps all devices (stages) busy much more consistently, significantly improving hardware utilization and overall training throughput.

Benefits:

- **Enables Training Very Large Models:** Like other forms of model parallelism, its primary benefit is allowing models exceeding single-device memory to be trained.

- **Improved Device Utilization (with Micro-batching):** Compared to a naive sequential

108

approach, micro-batching keeps the pipeline "full" and reduces device idle time.

- **Structured Approach:** Conceptually simpler to understand than some forms of tensor parallelism, resembling a natural workflow.

Considerations:

- **Communication Overhead:** Requires efficient transfer of activations (forward) and gradients (backward) between devices, which can be a bottleneck.

- **Load Balancing:** Partitioning the model into stages with roughly equal computational cost is crucial to prevent some stages from becoming bottlenecks while others wait.

- **Complexity:** Implementing efficient micro-batch scheduling and managing the pipeline dependencies requires sophisticated frameworks (like DeepSpeed, Megatron-LM, or PyTorch's pipeline parallel modules).

109

In essence, pipeline parallelism provides a structured way to divide large models across devices, functioning like an assembly line where micro-batching ensures continuous work flow and improved efficiency compared to processing entire batches sequentially through the stages.

By understanding and implementing these distributed training strategies, you can optimize the performance of your LLM training, ensuring that the process is both efficient and scalable.

3.25 Popular Distributed Training Frameworks

When it comes to distributed training frameworks, there are several popular options available that can help you efficiently train large language models (LLMs).

Horovod, developed by Uber, is a distributed training framework designed to make distributed deep learning fast and easy to use. It allows you to scale your training across multiple machines with minimal code changes.

110

DeepSpeed, developed by Microsoft, is another powerful distributed training framework. It is optimized for training large-scale models and offers various features to improve training speed and efficiency. DeepSpeed is designed to work seamlessly with PyTorch.

PyTorch DistributedDataParallel (DDP) is a built-in distributed training module in PyTorch. It provides a straightforward way to perform distributed training by parallelizing your model across multiple GPUs. DDP ensures that each GPU processes a portion of the data, leading to faster training times.

TensorFlow Distributed Training is a built-in module in TensorFlow that supports distributed training. It offers various strategies for distributing your model and data across multiple devices, making it easier to scale your training.

By utilizing these distributed training frameworks, you can optimize the training process for your LLM, ensuring efficient use of computational resources and faster training times. Each framework has its strengths and can be chosen based on your specific needs and preferences.

3.26 Example: Training on AWS SageMaker

AWS SageMaker is a cloud platform that simplifies the process of training large language models (LLMs). Imagine you're training an LLM on news articles from the past decade. SageMaker can distribute the workload across multiple EC2 instances, which are virtual computers in the cloud. For example, one instance might process articles from 2015, another from 2016, and so on. These instances share updates, allowing your model to train faster without losing accuracy.

To get started, you'll need to create a SageMaker Training Job. This involves specifying the training script, the type of instances you'll use, and the number of instances required. Next, configure distributed training using the SageMaker Distributed Training library. This helps in setting up data parallelism or model

112

parallelism, depending on your needs. Once everything is configured, launch the training job. SageMaker will automatically provision the necessary resources and start the training process. You can monitor the progress and performance metrics using the SageMaker console.

Understanding why this matters can put it all into perspective. Distributed training saves time and enables you to tackle large-scale projects. Companies like OpenAI use this approach to build massive models like ChatGPT. While this might be overkill for smaller tasks, knowing that such infrastructure exists highlights the flexibility and scalability of LLMs.

If you're just starting out, it's a good idea to try things locally first. Experiment on your laptop or use Google Colab. When you're ready to scale up, consider using AWS's free tier.

3.27 Overcoming Challenges (Troubleshooting and Optimization - The Chef's Toolkit)

Building LLMs isn't all smooth sailing. Here are two common hurdles and how developers dodge them.

One of the primary challenges is hardware limitations. Big models need big power, but not everyone has an A100 GPU lying around. The solution is to use GPUs when you can, even rented ones in the cloud, or stick to smaller models for practice. Every bit of speed helps and makes a noticeable difference in training times.

Another significant challenge is model size and speed. Some LLMs are slow and bulky, like a giant truck compared to a zippy scooter. A trick called knowledge distillation can shrink them down. It's like teaching a smaller model to mimic a big one, keeping the smarts but losing the weight. This makes the model faster and easier to run.

Efficient training techniques, like knowledge distillation, optimize model size and speed without compromising performance. Knowledge distillation involves training a

114

smaller "student" model to mimic the behavior of a larger "teacher" model, resulting in a more efficient model that performs similarly well.

A practical tip is to optimize early. Test your model's speed and size as you go. If it's sluggish, try distillation or simpler data—your users will thank you for a snappy tool.

And there you have it—the software infrastructure behind LLMs. From frameworks like NVIDIA's A100 to pre-trained models like BERT, from workflows to distributed training, these tools and processes are the unsung heroes making AI magic happen. Whether you're dreaming of a chatbot, a translator, or something totally new, understanding this foundation gives you the power to build it.

The best part? You don't need to be an expert to start. With free tools, cloud resources, and a bit of curiosity, you can dip your toes into this world. So go ahead— play with a model, tweak it, and see what you can create. The infrastructure is there to support you, and

115

who knows? Maybe your next project will change how we talk to machines.

116

CHAPTER 4: Data Acquisition and Management: Fueling Your LLM with the Right Data

The Lifeblood of LLMs

Hey there! Welcome to Chapter 4 of our LLM - Deep Dive adventure. So far, we've uncovered what large language models (LLMs) are, peeked at the hardware that powers them, and explored the software infrastructure behind their magic. Now, it's time to talk about something that ties it all together: data. If LLMs are the brain, data is the food that keeps them growing smart and strong.

Think about it—without words, sentences, or stories to learn from, an LLM wouldn't know how to chat with you or translate a sentence. Getting the right data isn't just a chore; it's a big part of the fun! In this chapter, we'll walk you through how to find, store, and manage data so your LLM can shine. We'll cover where to grab high-quality datasets, how to store them without losing your mind, ways to clean and boost your data, and some tricky challenges to watch out for. Plus, I'll toss in tips and examples to make it all feel doable—even if you're just starting out. Ready to fuel up your LLM? Let's go!

117

4.1 Understanding Your Data Needs: What Does Your LLM Need to Learn? (Setting the Table)

Before you start scouring the internet for data, it's important to understand what your LLM needs to learn. What tasks will it perform? What knowledge domain should it master? Defining your data needs upfront will save you time and effort in the long run. Think of it like planning a menu before going grocery shopping.

4.2 Defining the Task: What Will Your LLM Do? (The Main Course)

The first step in building a Large Language Model (LLM) is to clearly define the task it will perform. This helps in selecting the appropriate tools and techniques for training the model. Here are some examples of tasks that an LLM can handle.

Text generation involves creating realistic and coherent text, such as articles, stories, or poems. The LLM learns to predict the next word in a sentence, allowing it to create fluid and engaging text.

Question answering is another task that LLMs excel at. This involves providing accurate and relevant answers to questions based on a given context. The LLM

118

processes the context and generates responses that align with the information provided.

Translation is the process of converting text from one language to another. By learning the patterns and structures of multiple languages, an LLM can provide accurate translations, making it easier to communicate across language barriers.

Summarization involves condensing long texts into shorter, more concise versions. The LLM identifies the key points in the text and generates a summary that captures the main ideas without losing essential information.

Code generation is a valuable task for LLMs, where they generate code based on a natural language description. By understanding the requirements and context provided in plain language, the LLM can produce corresponding code snippets, aiding developers in their work.

Finally, chatbots engage in natural and informative conversations with users. The LLM can understand user

119

inputs, process the information, and generate appropriate responses to maintain a meaningful dialogue, enhancing the user experience.

By clearly defining the task your LLM will perform, you can tailor the training process and select the most suitable pre-trained models and frameworks. This ensures that your LLM is well-equipped to handle the specific requirements of the task at hand.

4.3 Identifying the Knowledge Domain: What Should Your LLM Know? (The Ingredients)

Once you've defined the task, the next step is to identify the knowledge domain that your Large Language Model (LLM) should master. This ensures that the model is equipped with the relevant information to perform its designated task effectively.

For general knowledge, the LLM should have a broad understanding of facts, concepts, and events across various subjects. This enables it to handle a wide range of topics and provide accurate information.

120

If the LLM is intended for a specific domain, such as medicine, law, or finance, it should have expertise in that particular field. This allows the model to understand and generate specialized content, making it a valuable tool for domain-specific tasks.

For programming-related tasks, the LLM should have knowledge of programming languages and software development. This includes understanding syntax, best practices, and common coding patterns to assist in tasks like code generation and debugging.

In the realm of creative writing, the LLM should be familiar with literary styles, techniques, and genres. This knowledge enables the model to generate engaging and coherent stories, poems, or other creative content.

For customer service applications, the LLM should understand common customer inquiries and solutions. This helps the model provide accurate and helpful responses, enhancing the user experience.

By identifying the appropriate knowledge domain, you ensure that your LLM is well-prepared to tackle the specific requirements of the task at hand. This targeted approach leads to more accurate and relevant outputs, making the LLM a powerful tool in your arsenal.

4.4 Matching Data to Task and Domain: Finding the Perfect Fit (The Recipe)

The next step in building your Large Language Model (LLM) is to find data that matches both the task and the knowledge domain. This ensures that the model is trained on relevant and high-quality data, leading to better performance.

For instance, if you're building a chatbot for a medical website, you will need data that covers medical topics and is suitable for conversational interactions. This could include medical articles, patient-doctor dialogues, and FAQs about medical conditions.

If you're creating a code generation model, you'll need a dataset of code examples and natural language descriptions. This helps the model understand how to

122

generate accurate code snippets based on the descriptions provided.

The goal is to find the right recipe that combines task-specific data with domain-specific knowledge. This combination allows your LLM to perform its designated task effectively and accurately.

A practical tip is to create a data requirements document. This document outlines the task, knowledge domain, and specific data characteristics needed for your LLM. It serves as a guide throughout the data acquisition and management process, ensuring that you collect and use the right data for training your model.

By carefully matching the data to the task and domain, you can optimize the training process and ensure that your LLM delivers high-quality results.

4.5 Where to Source High-Quality Data: Your Treasure Hunt Begins

Picture yourself as a treasure hunter, but instead of gold, you're after words, sentences, and stories. The first step in building an

123

LLM is finding the right data to teach it. Lucky for us, there are tons of places to look—some free, some custom-made. Let's check out the best spots.

Public Datasets: Ready-Made Goodies (Free Libraries)

The easiest place to start when training your Large Language Model (LLM) is with publicly available datasets. These datasets act like free libraries stuffed with text from all over the world. Big players like OpenAI have used datasets from sites like Kaggle, a hub for data enthusiasts, and arXiv, a collection of research papers, to train their models. You can take advantage of these resources too.

Common Crawl is a giant repository of web pages, including billions of words from blogs, news sites, and more. This provides a vast and diverse dataset for training your LLM.

C4, or the Colossal Clean Crawled Corpus, is a cleaner subset of Common Crawl. It removes much of the noise

124

and irrelevant content, making it a more refined dataset for training.

Wikipedia offers clean, organized articles on almost every topic imaginable. It's a great source of structured and reliable information for your model.

Books3 is a large collection of books that can enrich your LLM with literary content. However, be aware of potential copyright issues with this dataset and ensure you have the right to use the content.

The Pile is a diverse mix of books, code, and random internet text, providing a variety of content for training. This variety can help your model handle a wide range of topics and styles.

Kaggle Datasets offer a wide variety of datasets submitted by the Kaggle community. You can find data on numerous subjects, making it a versatile resource for training your LLM.

These public datasets are great because they're accessible and cover a vast array of topics. For example, if you want your LLM to chat about space, you can grab some arXiv papers. If you need it to sound casual, you can dig into the web scraps from Common Crawl.

A practical tip is to carefully review the license terms and usage restrictions when using public datasets. This ensures that you are complying with the applicable rules and can legally use the data for training your model.

By starting with these ready-made goodies, you can efficiently train your LLM and equip it with the knowledge it needs to perform effectively.

4.6 Academic Repositories: The Smart Stuff (Expert Knowledge)

If you want something a bit more polished for your Large Language Model (LLM), academic repositories are your best friends. Platforms like arXiv and the ACL Anthology offer high-quality text written by experts, making them ideal for training LLMs on specific topics

126

like medicine or tech. The data from these sources is both deep and reliable.

arXiv is a repository of electronic preprints of scientific papers in fields such as mathematics, physics, computer science, quantitative biology, statistics, and quantitative finance. This vast collection of research papers provides a rich source of well-structured and comprehensive data.

The ACL Anthology Network is another valuable resource, offering a comprehensive collection of research papers in the field of natural language processing. This repository covers a wide range of topics within NLP, providing high-quality, peer-reviewed content.

A practical tip when using academic datasets is to note that they are often well-curated and documented. This makes them a valuable resource for LLM training, ensuring that your model is trained on accurate and reliable data.

127

By leveraging these academic repositories, you can ensure that your LLM is built on a foundation of expert knowledge, leading to more precise and effective outputs.

4.7 Web Scraping: Extracting Data from the Web

Web scraping involves extracting data from websites using automated tools. This technique is particularly useful for collecting data that is not available in public datasets or academic repositories. Several tools can assist with web scraping, each with its own strengths and functionalities.

Beautiful Soup is a popular Python library for parsing HTML and XML. It is easy to use and excels at navigating and modifying parse trees, making it ideal for extracting data from web pages.

Scrapy is a robust Python framework designed specifically for building web scrapers. It provides a range of features and flexibility, allowing you to scrape large volumes of data efficiently. Scrapy is well-suited for complex scraping tasks and can handle a variety of data extraction needs.

Selenium is a tool for automating web browsers. It is commonly used for testing web applications, but it can also be leveraged for web scraping. Selenium allows you to interact with web pages, fill out forms, and navigate through websites, making it useful for scraping dynamic content.

When engaging in web scraping, it's important to be respectful of website terms of service and robots.txt files. These files indicate the rules and restrictions for web crawlers and should be adhered to. Additionally, avoid overloading websites with requests to prevent potential disruptions or bans. Always attribute the source of the data you collect, maintaining ethical practices in your web scraping activities.

By utilizing these web scraping tools and following best practices, you can gather valuable data to enhance the training of your LLM and ensure it is well-informed and capable.

129

4.8 Custom Datasets: Make Your Own (Tailor-Made Data)

Sometimes, you need something super specific—like reviews for a movie chatbot or tweets for a social media tool. That's when you roll up your sleeves and create your own dataset. You could scrape websites (legally, of course!), ask people to contribute, or even write some text yourself. For example, a small team once built a custom dataset of customer service chats to train a helpful bot—tailor-made perfection.

Creating custom datasets tailored to specific tasks can be a powerful strategy when public datasets fall short of requirements. This involves collecting data from various sources and curating it to meet the specific needs of your LLM.

There are several methods for creating custom datasets. Manual annotation involves labeling data by hand, ensuring accuracy and relevance. Crowdsourcing outsources data annotation to a large group of people, speeding up the process. Automated data generation

130

uses algorithms to create synthetic data, which can be useful for generating large amounts of data quickly.

When creating custom datasets, focus on quality over quantity. A smaller, well-curated dataset can often outperform a larger, poorly curated dataset. Starting with a small, free dataset—like a chunk of Wikipedia—can help you test your ideas without overwhelming yourself. Websites like Kaggle or Hugging Face offer samples you can download in minutes, making it easy to dip your toes in the water before jumping in.

By creating tailor-made datasets, you can ensure that your LLM is trained on the most relevant and accurate data for its specific task, leading to better performance and more reliable results.

4.9 Data Storage Solutions: Keeping It All Safe and Sound

Once you've got your data, you need a place to stash it. Imagine collecting a mountain of books—you'd need shelves, right? For LLMs, we're talking tons of text, so storage has to be smart, scalable, and easy to access.

131

Here's how it works. Storing large volumes of data efficiently is essential for maintaining performance and scalability. As LLMs and their training datasets grow, choosing the right storage solution becomes critical.

4.10 Cloud Storage: Your Digital Warehouse

Cloud services like AWS S3 (Amazon's storage) or Google Cloud Storage are like renting a big, flexible warehouse online. They grow with your needs, so if your dataset jumps from 1 GB to 100 GB, it's no problem. Plus, you can access your data from anywhere. For example, a startup might use AWS S3 to store movie reviews, scaling up as they add more—making the process simple and stress-free.

Leveraging cloud storage services like AWS S3 or Google Cloud Storage offers scalable solutions, ensuring data availability even as models grow. For instance, a startup might scale its data storage effectively using these services to handle expanding datasets without compromising accessibility.

132

The benefits of cloud storage include scalability, as it allows you to easily scale storage capacity up or down as needed. It offers accessibility, enabling you to access data from anywhere in the world. Cloud storage providers also offer high levels of data durability and redundancy, ensuring your data is safe and secure. Additionally, cloud storage is cost-effective, as you only pay for the storage you use.

When choosing a cloud storage provider, consider the features and pricing that best meet your needs. By selecting the right provider, you can ensure that your data storage is efficient, scalable, and cost-effective.

4.11 Distributed Systems: Teamwork Makes the Dream Work

For really huge datasets, think billions of words, the Hadoop Distributed File System (HDFS) is a champ. It splits your data across multiple computers, like handing out puzzle pieces to friends. If one computer crashes, the others keep going, and it's fast because everyone works together. Big companies use this to handle insane amounts of text without breaking a sweat.

133

Distributed systems such as HDFS provide robust solutions for managing large-scale data. By distributing data across multiple nodes, organizations can ensure redundancy and quick access, which are crucial for training complex models.

One of the major benefits of distributed file systems is scalability. They can handle massive datasets by distributing them across multiple nodes, making it easier to manage large volumes of data. Redundancy is another advantage, as distributed systems replicate data across multiple nodes, ensuring data availability even if some nodes fail.

Fault tolerance is a key feature of distributed file systems. They can continue to operate even if some nodes experience issues, maintaining the integrity and accessibility of the data. Additionally, distributed systems provide high throughput, offering high-speed data access for training models efficiently.

Consider using a distributed file system if you are working with very large datasets and need high levels

134

of scalability and reliability. This approach will help you manage your data effectively and ensure your models are trained on a robust and accessible dataset.

4.12 Local Storage: Keep It Close

If you're just starting out or want total control over your data, using your own computer or an external hard drive works perfectly fine. Local storage is great for small projects or sensitive data—like personal notes you don't want to store in the cloud. Just make sure to back it up! While cloud and distributed storage offer scalability, local storage can be beneficial when dealing with smaller projects or prioritizing data privacy.

Local storage offers several benefits. You have full control over your data and infrastructure, ensuring that you manage everything according to your preferences. Keeping sensitive data on-premises enhances privacy, as it remains under your direct supervision. Additionally, local storage provides low latency, meaning faster data access for training your models.

135

When using local storage, ensure you have adequate backup and disaster recovery plans. This way, you protect your data from potential loss or damage.

If you're new to this and want to explore cloud storage, many cloud providers offer free tiers. Services like AWS and Google Cloud give you a small chunk of storage to play with. Upload a dataset there and see how easy it is to access. It's a no-risk way to test the waters and decide if cloud storage suits your needs.

By considering these options, you can choose the best storage solution for your project, whether it's local storage for control and privacy or cloud storage for scalability and convenience.

4.13 Data Processing & Augmentation: Polishing Your Raw Materials

Okay, you've got your data—now what? Raw data is like a rough diamond; it needs some polishing to sparkle. This is where processing and augmentation come in—cleaning it up and making it even better for your LLM. Data processing is a vital step that involves cleaning,

136

transforming, and enhancing raw data to make it suitable for model training. It's like refining raw ore into precious metal.

4.14 Data Cleaning: Sweep Away the Mess

Raw text can be messy—typos, weird symbols, or duplicate lines. Cleaning it up means fixing those issues to ensure the data is usable. For example, if you grab web data, you might need to strip out HTML tags, correct spelling errors, or remove duplicate lines. There was a project where a jumbled forum dataset was transformed into clean, usable text, and suddenly, the LLM could actually learn from it.

Data cleaning involves removing irrelevant characters, HTML tags, and other noise from the data. It also involves correcting errors and inconsistencies to make the data more accurate and reliable.

Several techniques can help in the data cleaning process. Regular expressions are useful for removing unwanted characters and patterns. HTML parsing helps extract text from HTML documents. Spell checking corrects spelling errors, and data deduplication removes duplicate entries.

A practical tip is to automate your data cleaning process as much as possible. Automation reduces manual effort and ensures consistency across your dataset, making the entire process more efficient.

By investing time in data cleaning, you ensure that your LLM is trained on high-quality data, leading to better performance and more accurate results.

4.15 Tokenization: Chop It Up

Tokenization is like cutting a big sandwich into bite-sized pieces. It breaks text into words or smaller chunks, called tokens, so the LLM can process it more easily. One interesting method is Byte Pair Encoding (BPE), which starts with characters and builds common word parts, like "ing" or "un," to handle rare words. For example, if your dataset has the word "unbelievable," BPE might split it into "un" + "believ" + "able." Pretty neat, right?

138

Techniques like tokenization, using methods such as Byte Pair Encoding (BPE), break down text into manageable units, improving the model's ability to understand context. Tokenization involves splitting text into individual words or subwords, making it easier for the LLM to process and learn from the data.

There are different tokenization methods to consider. Word-based tokenization splits text into individual words. Subword tokenization breaks text into smaller units, such as morphemes or character n-grams. Byte Pair Encoding (BPE) is a subword tokenization algorithm that learns a vocabulary of common subword units, making it effective at handling rare words and out-of-vocabulary tokens.

When choosing a tokenization method, select one that is appropriate for your language and task. BPE is often a good choice for LLMs, as it can handle rare words and out-of-vocabulary tokens effectively.

By implementing tokenization, you ensure that your LLM can process and understand text more efficiently,

139

leading to better performance and more accurate results.

4.16 Data Augmentation: Add Some Spice

What if your data feels thin? Augmentation beefs it up! You could swap words with synonyms, translate text to another language and back again, or mix in community content—like forum posts from a contest. One team boosted their dataset with fan fiction to make their LLM more creative—variety is the key.

Data augmentation involves creating new data points from existing ones. This helps improve the performance and robustness of your LLM. For example, a project might augment its dataset by incorporating community-contributed content from contests or forums, enriching the data with diverse perspectives and experiences.

There are several techniques for data augmentation. Synonym replacement involves swapping words with their synonyms. Random insertion adds random words into the text. Random deletion removes random words

140

from the text. Back translation translates the text into another language and then back to the original language, introducing variations. Text paraphrasing rephrases sentences while preserving their meaning.

By using data augmentation techniques, you can increase the size and diversity of your training dataset. This leads to better performance and more robust models.

If you're unsure where to start, the Hugging Face datasets library is a beginner's dream. It's free, easy to use, and handles cleaning and tokenization for you. Try loading a small dataset there and playing with it—no coding PhD required.

With these techniques, you can ensure that your LLM is trained on a diverse and comprehensive dataset, enhancing its capabilities and making it more effective at performing its tasks.

4.17 Challenges & Considerations: Dodging the Pitfalls

Data sounds fun until you hit a snag. Don't worry— every LLM builder faces challenges. Let's tackle the big ones and keep your project on track. Data management often presents unique challenges. It's important to be aware of these challenges and take steps to mitigate them.

Data Privacy: Play It Safe

If you're using social media posts or personal chats, privacy is crucial. You can't just grab someone's tweets without permission! Laws like GDPR in Europe mean you need to anonymize data by stripping out names or details, or get consent. A smart move is to stick to public, anonymized datasets until you're ready to handle the legal aspects.

When handling user data from social media platforms, data privacy is paramount. Ensuring compliance with regulations while maintaining the integrity of your model is essential.

142

There are several techniques for protecting data privacy. Anonymization involves removing identifying information from the data. Differential privacy adds noise to the data to protect individual privacy, ensuring that the data remains useful while safeguarding sensitive information. Federated learning allows you to train models on decentralized data without sharing the data itself, preserving privacy while enabling collaborative training.

When dealing with data privacy, it's important to consult with legal experts to ensure that you are complying with all applicable regulations. By taking these steps, you can protect user privacy and maintain the integrity of your LLM.

4.18 Scalability: Plan for Growth

Your dataset might start small, but what if it grows rapidly? A local hard drive won't suffice for storing 10 terabytes of text. This is where cloud storage or HDFS comes into play, as they can scale with your needs. For instance, a team once outgrew their laptop storage

143

mid-project and shifted to AWS, which saved the day. Addressing scalability ensures that storage solutions can handle growth without compromising performance.

As your LLM project grows, you'll need to be able to scale your data pipeline to handle increasing amounts of data. This involves using scalable solutions that can grow with your needs, ensuring data availability and performance.

One technique for ensuring scalability is using cloud storage services, which can scale to meet your storage requirements. Cloud storage allows you to easily adjust your storage capacity, ensuring that you have enough space for your growing dataset.

Another technique is distributed processing, which involves using frameworks like Apache Spark to process data in parallel. Distributed processing can handle large volumes of data efficiently by dividing the workload across multiple nodes.

144

Data partitioning is another effective method. This involves dividing your data into smaller partitions that can be processed independently. Data partitioning improves processing speed and efficiency, making it easier to manage large datasets.

When designing your data pipeline, plan for scalability from the beginning. By considering scalability early on, you can ensure that your LLM project can handle growth without any hiccups, leading to a more robust and efficient data pipeline.

4.19 Quality: Garbage In, Garbage Out

Bad data leads to a bad LLM. If your text is full of errors or off-topic rants, your model will stumble. It's crucial to double-check your sources and clean ruthlessly. For instance, one coder found their model spouting nonsense because they forgot to filter out spam— lesson learned! Maintaining data quality is essential for training high-performing LLMs, as inaccurate or inconsistent data can lead to biased or unreliable models.

145

Ensuring data quality involves several techniques. Data validation is the process of checking that your data meets certain criteria. This step helps in identifying and correcting issues early. Data profiling involves using tools to identify potential data quality issues, giving you a clearer picture of the data's overall health. Data governance includes establishing policies and procedures to ensure data quality over time, making sure that your data remains accurate and reliable.

A practical tip is to regularly monitor your data quality and address any issues that arise. This proactive approach ensures that your LLM is always trained on high-quality data.

Another practical tip is to test early. Before committing to a large dataset, test a tiny batch of data. Feed it to a small model, like a mini-BERT from Hugging Face, and see the results. If it's gibberish, tweak your cleaning or source. It's better to catch and fix issues early on.

By focusing on data quality from the start, you can ensure that your LLM performs effectively, providing accurate and reliable outputs.

4.20 Tools & Libraries: Simplifying Data Handling (The Data Scientist's Toolbox)

To simplify data handling, tools and libraries like the Hugging Face datasets library provide user-friendly interfaces for managing diverse datasets efficiently. These resources empower developers to focus on innovation rather than low-level details.

One valuable tool is the Hugging Face Datasets library, which makes it easy to access and process a wide variety of datasets for natural language processing (NLP) tasks. This library streamlines the data handling process, allowing you to focus on building and fine-tuning your models.

Apache Spark is another powerful resource, offering a distributed processing framework for handling large datasets. Spark enables parallel processing across

147

multiple nodes, making it efficient for large-scale data analysis and training.

Dask is a parallel computing library for Python that can be used to process data in parallel on a single machine or on a cluster. Dask helps optimize computation and manage large datasets with ease.

Pandas is a widely-used Python library for data analysis and manipulation. It provides data structures and functions needed to clean and analyze data, making it a staple in the data scientist's toolbox.

For natural language processing tasks, NLTK and SpaCy are two popular Python libraries. NLTK provides a suite of tools for text processing, including tokenization, parsing, and more. SpaCy is known for its high performance and ease of use, making it ideal for building NLP applications.

By exploring different tools and libraries, you can find the ones that best fit your needs and workflow. Each tool offers unique capabilities that can simplify and

148

enhance your data handling processes, allowing you to focus on the more innovative aspects of your projects.

4.21 Best Practices: Lessons Learned from Successful Projects (The Data Whisperer's Guide)

Learning from successful projects, best practices include prioritizing open-source datasets, ensuring robust storage solutions, and leveraging community contributions to enhance data quality. By adopting these strategies, organizations can foster innovation while maintaining scalability and accessibility.

Starting with open-source datasets whenever possible is a smart move to reduce costs and avoid licensing issues. These datasets are freely available and can provide a solid foundation for your LLM project.

Choosing storage solutions that are scalable, reliable, and secure is crucial. This ensures that your data is always accessible and protected, even as your project grows.

Participating in the LLM community and contributing to open-source datasets and tools can enhance data quality and foster collaboration. By leveraging

150

community contributions, you can benefit from the collective knowledge and experience of others.

Automating as much of your data pipeline as possible reduces manual effort and ensures consistency. This leads to a more efficient and reliable process, allowing you to focus on the more innovative aspects of your project.

Implementing data quality monitoring procedures helps you identify and address potential issues early on. Regularly monitoring your data quality ensures that your LLM is trained on accurate and reliable data.

Always prioritize data privacy and ethical considerations when working with data. Adhering to ethical guidelines protects user privacy and maintains the integrity of your project.

Data acquisition and management might sound like a lot, but it's the secret sauce that makes LLMs amazing. From hunting down datasets on Kaggle to storing them in the cloud, from cleaning out the junk to dodging

151

privacy traps—you've got the tools to fuel your LLM right.

The cool part is that you don't need to be a data wizard to start. Grab a free dataset, play with Hugging Face, and experiment. Every step you take—whether it's tokenizing a sentence or scaling to AWS—builds your skills and your model. So, what's next? Dive in, get your hands dirty with data, and watch your LLM come to life. You've got this!

CHAPTER 5: The Training Process: A Step-by-Step Guide to Building Your LLM

5.1 Embarking on Your LLM Training Journey

Hey there, welcome to Chapter 5 of LLM - Deep Dive! By now, we've explored what large language models (LLMs) are, the hardware and software that power them, and how to gather the data they need. Now, it's time to roll up our sleeves and dive into the heart of it all: training your very own LLM. This chapter is your friendly roadmap through the training process—think of it as a recipe book for baking a smart, language-savvy model.

Training an LLM might sound like a big, scary task, but don't worry—we're breaking it down into simple, doable steps. Whether you're starting from scratch or tweaking an existing model, we'll walk you through setting up your tools, building the model, feeding it with data, and making sure it's learning the right way. Along the way, I'll share practical tips and examples to keep

153

things fun and manageable, even if you're new to this. Ready to turn your LLM dreams into reality? Let's get cooking!

5.2 Setting Up Your Development Environment: Getting the Kitchen Ready

Before we start training, we need to set up our workspace—like prepping the kitchen before baking a cake. A good setup saves time, avoids messes, and makes everything run smoothly. Let's look at what you'll need.

154

5.3 Hardware: Your Cooking Tools

Training a Large Language Model (LLM) takes some serious power, so let's talk about the essential hardware.

GPUs are the heavy lifters, like a super-fast oven. NVIDIA GPUs have special tensor cores that crunch numbers incredibly fast, making them perfect for the complex math behind LLMs. Without them, training could take forever. NVIDIA GPUs with multiple compute capabilities are critical for accelerated computations, as these GPUs are optimized for matrix operations, which are central to neural network training. Training an LLM involves processing large amounts of data, and GPUs can perform these tasks much faster than CPUs. If you don't have powerful GPUs, consider using cloud-based GPU instances.

TPUs, or Tensor Processing Units, developed by Google, are another option. Think of them as a specialized grill for AI tasks. They're excellent for certain calculations and are available on Google Cloud. TPUs offer superior

155

performance for specific types of computations, including those involved in training language models. They are optimized for the operations required for deep learning tasks, making them an excellent choice for LLM training. TPUs are primarily available through the Google Cloud Platform.

Your computer's brain (CPU) and memory (RAM) handle lighter jobs, like running code or loading data. While not as critical as GPUs or TPUs, a powerful CPU can manage lightweight tasks such as managing code and interacting with external systems during development. CPUs provide flexibility in handling non-computationally intensive tasks, while GPUs and TPUs focus on the heavy lifting. Ensure you have an adequate amount of RAM for your training tasks.

Fast SSDs (Solid State Drives) are like your pantry— quickly grabbing data so your model doesn't wait around. Fast storage is essential for quickly loading data during training. Slow storage can become a bottleneck and significantly slow down the training process.

By understanding and utilizing the right hardware, you can ensure that your LLM training is efficient and effective.

5.4 Software: Your Recipe Book

Next, let's grab the programs you'll use for developing your Large Language Model (LLM).

Python is the go-to language for AI—simple and packed with helpful tools. It is the preferred programming language for LLM development due to its simplicity and extensive libraries. Python's syntax is intuitive, making it an ideal choice for rapid prototyping and experimentation.

Using a virtual environment to manage your Python dependencies can help you avoid conflicts. To get started, first ensure that Python is installed on your system. You can check this by typing `python --version` or `python3 --version` in your terminal. If Python is not installed, you can easily install it by following the instructions on the official Python

157

website. Use the following set of commands to install in WSL or Linux Environment.

```
sudo apt update
sudo apt install python3
sudo apt install python3-pip
```

Create a Virtual Environment: It's a good practice to use a virtual environment for your Python projects to keep dependencies isolated. You can create a virtual environment using:

```
python3 -m venv myenv
source myenv/bin/activate
```

5.5 PyTorch or TensorFlow: Your Cooking Frameworks

These are your cooking frameworks—PyTorch is great for experimenting, while TensorFlow shines for big projects. Pick one and install it with a quick

```
pip install torch or pip install tensorflow
```

158

PyTorch and TensorFlow provide robust tools for building, training, and evaluating deep learning models. They are widely used in the research community and offer flexibility, scalability, and extensive documentation. JAX is a newer framework gaining popularity for its performance and composability.

Choose a framework that aligns with your expertise and project requirements. PyTorch is often preferred for research due to its intuitive design and dynamic computation graph. TensorFlow is favored for production deployment because of its scalability and robust ecosystem.

To install PyTorch, make sure you have your virtual environment activated. You can find the appropriate installation command on the PyTorch website. For example, you might use:

```
pip install torch torchvision torchaudio

pip install tensorflow

pip install jax
```

159

Run Python Code: Now you can run your Python code within this virtual environment. Create a new Python script or open a Python interpreter:

```
python
```

Import Torch: Within the Python interpreter or script, you can now import PyTorch:

```
import torch

print(torch.cuda.is_available())
```

These frameworks provide robust tools for building, training, and evaluating deep learning models.

Why they matter: TensorFlow and PyTorch are widely used in the research community and offer flexibility, scalability, and extensive documentation.

160

Practical Tip: Choose a framework that aligns with your expertise and project requirements.

5.6 Jupyter Notebooks

Jupyter Notebooks are like a digital scratch pad—perfect for testing ideas. You can install them with a simple command: `pip install notebook.`

Jupyter Notebooks provide an interactive environment for experimentation. They allow you to write, test, and visualize code all in one interface. This makes it easy to experiment with different hyperparameters, visualize model behavior, and debug issues.

While Jupyter Notebooks are excellent for prototyping and experimentation, it's also worth considering a more structured development environment like VS Code or PyCharm for larger projects. These environments offer additional features and tools that can help manage more complex codebases effectively.

By using Jupyter Notebooks, you can easily test and iterate on your ideas, making them an essential tool for any data scientist or developer working with LLMs.

5.7 Git: Your Recipe Binder

Commands:

```
sudo apt update
sudo apt install git
```

Git keeps your work organized and safe, much like a recipe binder. Setting up a GitHub repository allows you to track everything and manage your code efficiently.

Git is the standard tool for version control, allowing you to track changes to your project files. It provides a way to manage your code, collaborate with others, and maintain a clear history of your work. Version control systems enable collaboration, rolling back changes, and maintaining a clear history of your work.

Here's a step-by-step guide to get you started with Git:

162

First, install Git if you don't have it installed already. You can check if it's installed by typing **git --version** in your terminal. If it's not installed, you can download and install it from the official Git website.

Next, configure Git by setting up your user name and email. These details will be associated with your commits. You can do this by running the following commands in your terminal:

```
git config -global user.name "Your Name"

git config -global user.email
    "your.email@example.com"
```

3. Create a New Directory: Create a directory for your project if you don't already have one:

```
mkdir my_project
cd my_project
```

4. Initialize a Git Repository: Initialize a new Git repository in your project directory:

```
git init
```

163

5. Add Files: Add the files you want to track in your repository:

```
git add
```

6. Commit Changes: Commit your changes with a descriptive message:

```
git commit -m "Initial commit"
```

7. Connect to a Remote Repository: If you have a remote repository (e.g., on GitHub, GitLab,   Bitbucket), you can add it as a remote. Replace the URL with your repository's URL:

```
git remote add origin
https://github.com/username/my_project.git
```

8. Push Changes to Remote: Push your changes to the remote repository:

```
git push -u origin master
```

5.8 CUDA Toolkit: Essential for GPU Acceleration

The CUDA Toolkit provides the necessary drivers and libraries for using NVIDIA GPUs with deep learning frameworks. It is essential for enabling GPU

164

acceleration during training, which significantly speeds up the process.

To ensure optimal performance, make sure you have the correct version of the CUDA Toolkit installed for your specific GPU and deep learning framework. You can download the latest version of the CUDA Toolkit from the NVIDIA Developer website, where detailed installation instructions for various platforms are provided. If you require an older version, you can find it in the CUDA Toolkit Archive.

By having the right CUDA Toolkit version installed, you can take full advantage of GPU acceleration, leading to more efficient and faster training of your LLM.

5.9 Hugging Face Transformers Library

The Hugging Face Transformers library provides access to a wide range of pre-trained Large Language Models (LLMs) and tools for fine-tuning and training them. This library simplifies working with LLMs and offers access to many resources, making it easier to develop and experiment with models.

165

To acquire the Hugging Face Transformers Library, follow these steps:

First, ensure you have Python installed. You can check this by running **python --version** or **python3 --version** in your terminal. If Python is not installed, you can download it from the official Python website.

Next, create a virtual environment for your Python projects to keep dependencies isolated. This is a good practice to avoid conflicts. You can create a virtual environment using:

```
python3 -m venv myenv
source myenv/bin/activate
```

Install Transformers Library: Once you have your virtual environment activated, you can install the Transformers library using pip:

```
pip install transformers
```

Verify Installation: To check if the Transformers library is properly installed, you can run the following command:

166

```
python -c "from transformers import pipeline; print(pipeline('sentiment-
analysis')('This is a great example!'))"
```

5.10 Project Repository Initialization: Setting Up Your Workspace (Your Organized Workspace)

Organizing your project files is critical for managing large-scale training projects. A well-structured repository makes collaboration easier and ensures that you can always backtrack if something goes wrong.

GitHub and GitLab are excellent platforms for hosting open-source projects and collaborating with others. They provide a user-friendly interface for version control, file sharing, and project management. Creating a repository on GitHub or GitLab for your LLM project and using Git to track your changes can streamline your workflow.

Git is essential for managing your repository. It helps track changes at the file level and is crucial for maintaining large codebases. Git provides a robust way to track changes, revert to previous states, and work on multiple branches simultaneously.

Here's a suggested directory structure for organizing your project:

- **data/**: Store your training, validation, and test datasets here.
- **models/**: Store your model architecture and pre-trained weights.
- **scripts/**: Store your training, evaluation, and data preprocessing scripts.
- **notebooks/**: Store your Jupyter Notebooks for experimentation.
- **results/**: Store your training logs, evaluation metrics, and model checkpoints.

By setting up a well-organized workspace, you can manage your LLM project more efficiently and ensure that you have a clear structure to follow throughout the development process.

5.11 Troubleshooting Tips: Addressing Common Issues (When Things Go Wrong)

Ensuring that your system meets the hardware requirements for training is essential. If you're using cloud services, check their GPU or TPU availability.

Inconsistent hardware can lead to errors or suboptimal performance during training. Make sure to check the documentation for your deep learning framework and cloud provider to ensure that your hardware is compatible.

Memory management is crucial, especially when working with large models. Be mindful of memory usage and use tools like `nvidia-smi` on NVIDIA GPUs or cloud platforms that manage memory efficiently. Memory is a limiting factor in model training, and overloading your system can lead to crashes. If you are running out of memory, consider reducing the batch size or using gradient accumulation to simulate a larger batch size.

Software compatibility is another important aspect to consider. Verify that all installed software packages are compatible with each other and up-to-date. Incompatible versions of libraries can lead to runtime errors or unexpected behavior during training. Using a virtual environment to isolate your project dependencies can help ensure that you are using compatible versions of all libraries.

CUDA errors can be particularly challenging to troubleshoot if you are using NVIDIA GPUs. These errors are necessary to work with NVIDIA GPUs, so make sure you have the correct version of the CUDA Toolkit installed for your GPU and deep learning framework.

By addressing these common issues, you can ensure a smoother training process and improve the performance of your LLM.

```
nvcc --version # Ensure NVCC is accessible
nvidia-smi # Confirm GPU usage is detected
```

5.12 Building Your Model: Designing the Blueprint

With your kitchen ready, it's time to design your LLM—like sketching the blueprint for a house. This step is about picking its shape and setting it up to learn. Once your environment is set up, the next step is to initialize your model. This involves defining its architecture, parameters, and other critical components.

170

5.13 Understanding the Transformer: The Super-Smart Librarian

Most LLMs use a transformer design, inspired by the "Attention is All You Need" paper. It's like a super-smart librarian who can read a book and remember how every word connects. Large language models are typically based on transformer architectures, which process input sequences by applying self-attention mechanisms to capture long-range dependencies in text.

Key parts:

The **embedding layer** turns words into numbers the model understands—like translating "cat" into a secret code. This layer converts input tokens into dense vectors. Token embeddings are the foundation of the model's ability to understand and generate language. Using pre-trained word embeddings like Word2Vec, GloVe, or FastText can improve performance, especially when working with limited data.

The **transformer blocks** are where the magic happens. These layers use self-attention to figure out which

171

words matter most in a sentence (e.g., "cat" and "purr" go together). Each transformer block learns to represent the input at different levels of granularity, enabling the model to capture hierarchical patterns in text. Experiment with different numbers of transformer blocks to find the optimal balance between model complexity and performance.

The **output layer** spits out predictions—like guessing the next word in "The cat ___." This layer produces predictions for each token in the output sequence. The final layer transforms the processed embeddings into a probability distribution over possible outputs. Using a softmax activation function in the output layer ensures that the predictions are a valid probability distribution.

In most LLMs, the last layer includes a softmax activation function. Think of it this way: the LLM comes up with a list of "scores" for all the possible next words (like "slept," "ate," "jumped," etc.). These scores are just numbers, and the higher the number, the more the model thinks that word is a good fit. The softmax function takes those scores and turns them into

172

probabilities—like percentages. It makes sure that all the percentages add up to 100%. So, it might say: "Slept": 65% likely, "Ate": 25% likely, "Jumped": 10% likely. The softmax helps the model decide which word to pick and also gives you a sense of how confident the model is in its choice. In technical terms, the softmax function converts a list of raw scores into a list of probabilities, where each probability is between 0 and 1, and all the probabilities add up to 1.

The softmax function is key to understanding the confidence of the model's output and predicting the next value. It ensures that the output probabilities all add up to 1, which is necessary for many classification algorithms. The softmax function is also differentiable, which helps enhance backpropagation within neural networks.

Example: *Imagine a situation where you wanted to use neural networks and the softmax function to see if an image contains a cat, dog, or bird. The softmax function would output the probabilities for each image. So, a cat*

173

image might display the following probabilities: Cat: 65%
likely, Dog: 25% likely, Bird: 10% likely.

Code Implementation - PyTorch (Example):

This example provides example code using Pytorch for this step:

```python
import torch
import torch.nn.functional as F

# Example input tensor (logits)
logits = torch.tensor([2.0, 1.0, 0.1])

# Apply softmax
probabilities = F.softmax(logits, dim=0)

print(probabilities)
# Output: tensor([0.6590, 0.2424, 0.0986])
```

This demonstrates how softmax converts logits into probabilities.

5.14 Starting Smart: Initialization (Setting the Dials)

Your model begins with random numbers for its settings (called parameters). Think of it like setting the dials on an oven before baking—you don't want them too high or too low. Initialization of model parameters plays a crucial role in training performance. Poor

174

initialization can lead to issues like vanishing or exploding gradients, while good initialization helps the model converge faster.

There are two main tricks for initialization:

Random Initialization: This involves using small random numbers (like 0.02) to get started. Parameters are typically initialized with small random values, often from a normal distribution with a mean of 0 and a standard deviation of 0.02. Proper initialization allows the network to learn effectively from the input data.

Xavier Initialization: This is a more sophisticated method that balances things based on your model's size, keeping it stable as it learns. This method adjusts the scale of the initial weights based on the number of input and output units, helping prevent gradient issues in deep networks. It ensures that activations have consistent variance across layers, facilitating stable training.

175

By setting the dials correctly with these initialization techniques, you can help your model learn effectively and converge faster, leading to better performance.

5.15 Choosing Your Model Architecture

Now that you have a basic understanding of the Transformer, you need to choose the details of your model. Think of this as choosing the layout and features of the house you are building—you need to think about what you need and ensure that the model has the right parameters.

When designing your model architecture, consider the number of layers. Think of these layers as floors in a building. Each layer adds complexity and can help the model learn more intricate patterns in the data. Imagine that the higher the number of layers, the more knowledge someone has of the subject. More layers can capture more complex patterns but may lead to increased computational complexity and memory usage. Deeper models require more resources but can achieve better performance if properly optimized.

176

However, more is not always better—too many layers can make the model difficult to build and train.

Attention mechanisms are the tools the model uses to focus on the most important parts of the input. There are different types of attention mechanisms. Self-attention allows the model to look at different parts of the same input sentence to understand the relationships between words, much like reading a book and re-reading a sentence to understand it better. Cross-attention enables the model to focus on different sources of information. For example, in a translation task, the model might focus on the input sentence and the target language to generate accurate translations. Attention mechanisms determine how the model processes and combines information from different parts of the input sequence, and different types of attention mechanisms can be used depending on the task.

Tokenization and vocabulary size are also important considerations. Think of tokens as individual words or pieces of words, and the vocabulary is the list of all the

177

unique tokens the model knows. If the model doesn't know a word, it has no way to understand or generate it. A larger vocabulary can capture more nuances in language but increases memory usage and computational complexity. Choose a tokenization strategy that best suits your data. The size of the vocabulary directly impacts the model's ability to generalize.

By carefully considering these aspects, you can design a model architecture that is well-suited to your needs and capable of achieving optimal performance.

5.16 Practical Tip: Use a Pre-Made Blueprint

Don't want to build from scratch? Grab a pre-trained model from Hugging Face (like "distilbert-base-uncased"). It's like using a cake mix—you just tweak it for your flavor.

Step 1: Set Up Your Environment

Before you can run the code, you need a place to write and execute it. Think of this as setting up your kitchen before baking.

Install Python (essential)

Python is the language this code uses—it's beginner-friendly and powers most AI tools.

How to Install Python:

1) Go to python.org
2) Download the latest version (e.g., 3.11 as of February 2025).
3) Run the installer. Check the box to "Add Python to PATH" during setup—this makes it easy to use.
4) Open a terminal (Command Prompt on Windows, Terminal on Mac/Linux) and type `python --version`. If you see a version number, you're golden!

Install a Code Editor (Optional but Helpful)

179

A code editor is like having a recipe book with a built-in timer—it makes coding easier.

How to Install a Code Editor:

Download Visual Studio Code (VS Code). It's free. Install it, then add the Python extension (search "Python" in the extensions tab).

Use Google Colab (Easiest Option)

If installing stuff feels daunting, Colab is a free, cloud-based tool with everything pre-set—no downloads needed!

How to Use Google Colab:

Go to colab.google, sign in with a Google account, and click "New Notebook." You'll get a blank coding page with a "Run" button—perfect for beginners.

Step 2: Install the Hugging Face Transformers Library

180

The code uses the transformers library from Hugging Face—it's your cake mix supplier. You need to install it.

On Your Computer:

1. Open your terminal.
2. Type: `pip install transformers` and press Enter.
3. Wait a minute—it'll download the library. If it says "Successfully installed," you're set!

Running Python Code in the Python Interpreter:

Method 1

1. Open your command prompt or terminal.
2. Type `python` and press Enter to start the Python interpreter.
3. You should see the Python prompt (>>>). Now, you can type your Python code.

By following these steps, you can quickly set up your environment and start experimenting with pre-trained models from Hugging Face, making the process of building your LLM more manageable and efficient.

181

```
import transformers
print('Ready!')
```

Method 2

1. Open a text editor and create a new text file with a `.py` extension (e.g., `test_script.py`).
2. Write your Python code in the file.
3. Save the file.
4. In your command prompt or terminal, navigate to where you saved the file.

5. Run the script by typing **python test_script.py** and press enter. Ready should be returned. Move on to the next activity.

Step 1 Install the `transformers` Library (requirement).

Ensure you have the **transformers** library installed.
If you haven't installed it yet, you can do so using pip from command prompt or terminal shell:

```
pip install transformers
```

Step 2: Create a Python Script

182

Open a text editor and create a new Python file (e.g., run_distilbert.py),

Copy the following code into the file:

```
from transformers import DistilBertModel

model = DistilBertModel.from_pretrained("distilbert-base-uncased")
print("Model loaded successfully!")
```

In Google Colab

Step 3: Run the Python Script

1. Save the file.

2. Open your command prompt or terminal.

3. Navigate to the directory where you saved the file.

4. Run the script by typing:

```
python run_distilbert.py
```

You should see the message "Model loaded successfully!" indicating that the DistilBert model has been loaded correctly.

Step 4: Using an Interactive Python Session (Alternative Method)

183

You can also run the code directly in an interactive Python session:

1. Open your command prompt or terminal.
2. Start the Python interpreter by typing `python` and pressing Enter.
3. Enter the code line by line:

```
from transformers import DistilBertModel
```

You've successfully loaded the DistilBert model using the `transformers` library. Now, let's explore how to use this model for practical tasks like generating text embeddings or making predictions.

Step 1: Installing Necessary Libraries

Ensure you have the `transformers` and `torch` libraries installed. If not, you can install them using pip:

```
pip install transformers torch
```

Step 2: Loading the Model and Tokenizer

You need both the model and a tokenizer. The tokenizer converts text into numerical data that the

184

model can process. Open **run_distilburt.py** in a text
editor and replace the file with the following:

```python
from transformers import DistilBertModel, DistilBertTokenizer

# Load the tokenizer
tokenizer = DistilBertTokenizer.from_pretrained("distilbert-base-uncased")

# Load the model
model = DistilBertModel.from_pretrained("distilbert-base-uncased")
```

Step 3: Tokenizing Text

Convert your text into tokens that the model can
understand. Add the following into the
run_distilburt.py file:

```python
text = "Hello, how are you?"
inputs = tokenizer(text, return_tensors="pt")
```

Step 4: Making Predictions

Use the model to generate embeddings
(representations) of your input text by adding the

```
# Generate embeddings
outputs = model(**inputs)
last_hidden_states = outputs.last_hidden_state
print(last_hidden_states)
```

following to the **run_distilburt.py** text file:

Before running the **python run_distilburt.py** script
enter the following command to set the environment
variable to prevent error messages:

```
set TF_ENABLE_ONEDNN_OPTS=0
```

Run the script by navigating to your save location in
command prompt or *terminal* and entering **python
run_distilburt.py**

186

The full script should look like this once completed.

```python
from transformers import DistilBertModel, DistilBertTokenizer

# Load the tokenizer
tokenizer = DistilBertTokenizer.from_pretrained("distilbert-base-uncased")

# Load the model
model = DistilBertModel.from_pretrained("distilbert-base-uncased")

# Define your text
text = "Hello, how are you?"

# Tokenize the text
inputs = tokenizer(text, return_tensors="pt")

# Generate embeddings
outputs = model(**inputs)
last_hidden_states = outputs.last_hidden_state

# Print the embeddings
print(last_hidden_states)
```

Output of the script:

```
C:\Users\    \Documents>python run_distilbert.py
tensor([[[-2.2719e-01, -1.7390e-01, -5.0350e-02,  ..., -3.4869e-02,
           5.0236e-01,  3.4458e-01],
         [-2.0414e-02, -1.6917e-01,  3.8591e-01,  ...,  8.9658e-02,
           7.3483e-01,  4.7231e-04],
         [-6.1600e-01,  1.6398e-01,  5.8012e-01,  ..., -2.7803e-01,
           4.1833e-01,  2.3169e-01],
         ...,
         [-2.0863e-01, -8.6781e-01,  5.3058e-01,  ...,  3.3449e-01,
           5.8673e-01, -2.3773e-01],
         [-3.7604e-01, -6.4697e-01, -3.0601e-01,  ..., -2.0242e-01,
           6.0294e-01,  2.2844e-01],
         [ 7.9708e-01,  1.9524e-01, -4.4445e-01,  ...,  3.5078e-01,
          -3.4025e-01, -3.3902e-01]]], grad_fn=<NativeLayerNormBackward0>)
```

187

What Just Happened?

You ran a Python script using a pre-trained model called DistilBERT to generate embeddings (a type of numerical representation) from a sentence. Here's the whole process in simpler terms:

What's an Embedding?

Think of an embedding as a unique fingerprint for a piece of text. It's a way to turn words and sentences into numbers that a computer can understand and process.

The Process

1. **Loading the Model and Tokenizer:** You used a special tool called DistilBERT that has been trained to understand and generate human language. To use this tool, you first need to load it into your script.

2. **Tokenizing Text:** Before the tool can process the text, it needs to break it down into smaller units

188

called tokens. These tokens are like puzzle pieces that the tool can work with.

3. **Generating Embeddings:** Once the text is tokenized, the tool processes these tokens and generates embeddings. These embeddings are high-dimensional vectors (a fancy way of saying a list of numbers) that represent the text in a way that the computer can understand.

189

What Did the Output Look Like?

The output was a tensor, which is a multi-dimensional array of numbers.

Breaking Down the Output

- **Tensor:** It's a fancy word for a list of lists of numbers. Each list corresponds to a token in your input text.

- **Each Number:** These numbers are the embedding values that represent the meaning of the text. Think of them as coordinates in a high-dimensional space that uniquely identify your text.

- **Gradient Function** (`grad_fn`): This part is related to training the model and can be ignored for now. It's just an indicator that the tensor is part of a computational graph.

Why Does It Matter?

190

These embeddings can be used for various tasks like understanding the sentiment of a sentence (happy, sad, neutral), translating text, generating new text, and more. They help computers understand and work with human language more effectively.

You can easily acquire the Hugging Face Transformers Library by following these steps:

What to Install	What and How to Set it Up
To Install Python	sudo apt update sudo apt install python3
Python's Package Manager (pip)	sudo apt install python3-pip
PyTorch and Frameworks	pip install torch torchvision torchaudio
Libraries	You can easily download any of the following libraries that will help you implement your projects!
Use PIP	As your default, use pip install <package>

191

CHAPTER 6: Optimization Techniques for Efficient Training: Supercharging Your LLM

Introduction: Level Up Your LLM Training

Hey there, welcome to Chapter 6 of our LLM - Deep Dive! By now, you've set up your tools, built your model, fed it data, and started training. But what if your LLM could learn faster, use less power, and perform even better? That's where optimization techniques come in—like giving your model a turbo boost to zoom past obstacles and reach its full potential.

Optimization is all about making training smarter, not harder. In this chapter, we'll explore some cool tricks to tweak your setup, save memory, speed things up, and smooth out the learning process. Think of it as tuning a car: a little adjustment here and there can make a huge difference. We'll keep it simple with everyday examples and handy tips, so even if you're new to this, you'll feel like a pro by the end. Ready to level up your LLM game? Let's dive in!

Optimization is a cornerstone of training large language models (LLMs), enabling both performance and efficiency. This chapter explores effective strategies to enhance the effectiveness and scalability of LLM training through various optimization

192

techniques. We'll explore a variety of techniques, from fine-tuning hyperparameters to leveraging advanced parallelization strategies.

6.1 Hyperparameter Tuning: Finding the Perfect Recipe

Imagine baking cookies—you've got sugar, flour, and butter, but the amounts matter. Too much sugar, and they're sickly sweet; too little flour, and they fall apart. In LLM training, hyperparameters are like those ingredients: settings like learning rate, batch size, and dropout that control how your model learns. Let's look at three ways to find the perfect mix.

Hyperparameters are crucial knobs that define how an LLM is trained, influencing its performance and convergence. Common hyperparameters include learning rates, batch sizes, regularization parameters like dropout rates, and the number of layers in the model. They're like the ingredients in a recipe: getting the right balance is key to a delicious result.

193

6.2 Grid Search: Try Everything

Picture testing every possible cookie recipe—1 tsp sugar with 2 cups flour, then 1.5 tsp sugar with 2.5 cups flour, and so on. Grid search does that for hyperparameters, trying every combo you give it. It's thorough but slow—great for small projects, not so much when you've got tons of options.

Imagine tuning a recipe for baking cookies—trying every combination of sugar, butter, and flour to find the perfect blend. Grid search exhaustively tests all possible hyperparameter values within predefined ranges. While thorough, it can be computationally expensive when dealing with many variables. It's like trying every single combination of settings on your car stereo until you find the perfect sound.

Practical Tip: Grid search is best suited for small hyperparameter spaces. If you have many hyperparameters to tune, consider using a more efficient technique like random search or Bayesian optimization.

194

Code Example (using scikit-learn):

```python
from sklearn.model_selection import GridSearchCV
from sklearn.svm import SVC
param_grid = {'C': [0.1, 1, 10], 'gamma': [0.1, 1, 10]}
grid = GridSearchCV(SVC(), param_grid, refit=True, verbose=2)
grid.fit(X_train, y_train)
print(grid.best_estimator_)
```

The script performs a grid search to find the best combination of hyperparameters (C and gamma) for the Support Vector Classifier. It tests each combination, evaluates the performance, and then prints the best model configuration.

This way, the script helps optimize the model for better performance by selecting the most suitable hyperparameters.

6.3 Random Search: Roll the Dice

Now imagine tossing random amounts of sugar and flour into the mix and tasting the results. Random search picks hyperparameter values by chance within a range—like 0.001 to 0.1 for learning rate. It's faster than

195

grid search and often finds a good spot without testing everything.

Instead of trying every possible combination like grid search, random search samples hyperparameters randomly from a predefined distribution. This method often requires fewer trials and is more efficient, especially in high-dimensional spaces where many parameters are involved. It's like throwing darts at a board with all the possible settings, hoping to hit the bullseye sooner.

Practical Tip: Random search is a good starting point for hyperparameter tuning. It's often more efficient than grid search, especially when you have many hyperparameters.

196

Code Example (using scikit-learn):

```
from sklearn.model_selection import RandomizedSearchCV
from scipy.stats import uniform
param_distributions = {'C': uniform(0.1, 10), 'gamma': uniform(0.1, 10)}
random_search = RandomizedSearchCV(SVC(), param_distributions, refit=True,
verbose=2, n_iter=10)
random_search.fit(X_train, y_train)
print(random_search.best_estimator_)
```

The script performs a randomized search to find the best combination of hyperparameters (C and gamma) for the Support Vector Classifier. Instead of trying every possible combination like grid search, it samples random combinations from the specified distributions and evaluates their performance, then prints the best model configuration.

This method is often faster than grid search and can still find good hyperparameters, especially when dealing with many parameters.

6.4 Bayesian Optimization: The Smart Helper

Think of a baking coach who says, "Last time, 1 tsp sugar worked well, so let's try 1.2 tsp next." Bayesian optimization uses past tries to guess what'll work best,

197

balancing new ideas with proven winners. It's like having a GPS for tuning—smart and efficient.

Picture guiding your friend to find the best path through a maze using hints about promising paths based on past attempts. Bayesian optimization uses probabilistic models to suggest optimal hyperparameters by learning from previous results. It balances exploring new possibilities and exploiting known good options, making it ideal for complex landscapes. It's like having a GPS for hyperparameter tuning, guiding you towards the optimal settings based on past performance.

Practical Tip: Bayesian optimization is a powerful technique, but it can be more complex to implement than grid search or random search. Consider using a library like Optuna or Hyperopt to simplify the process.

198

Code Example (using Optuna):

```python
import optuna
def objective(trial):
    C = trial.suggest_float('C', 0.1, 10)
    gamma = trial.suggest_float('gamma', 0.1, 10)
    model = SVC(C=C, gamma=gamma)
    model.fit(X_train, y_train)
    return model.score(X_val, y_val)
study = optuna.create_study(direction='maximize')
study.optimize(objective, n_trials=10)
print(study.best_params)
```

The script uses Optuna to efficiently search for the best values of the hyperparameters C and gamma for an SVC model. By trying different combinations of these hyperparameters and evaluating their performance, Optuna helps identify the most effective settings to maximize the model's accuracy.

By carefully tuning these hyperparameters, you can achieve better model performance and faster convergence tailored to specific tasks. Remember to validate your hyperparameters on a separate validation set to avoid overfitting to the training data.

6.5 Tuning Tip: Starting Simple with Random Search

New to hyperparameter tuning and feeling overwhelmed? Don't fall into the trap of overcomplicating things right away. A great starting point is **random search**. It's surprisingly effective, easy to implement, and a fantastic way to get a feel for how different hyperparameters affect your model's performance. Think of it like this: you're trying to unlock a combination lock, but you don't know the numbers. Instead of systematically trying every possible combination (like grid search), random search has you randomly spinning the dial and trying a few combinations. You might stumble upon the right one faster than you think!

6.6 How to Implement Random Search (Simplified Examples)

- **Using Hugging Face's Trainer:** The Hugging Face Trainer provides a convenient way to perform random search. Specify a search space (a range of values) for the hyperparameters you want to tune, and let the Trainer run multiple

200

training runs with randomly sampled values from that space.

Imagine you're building a race car (your machine learning model). The car's engine (the model's algorithm) is pretty good, but you want it to go faster. You can tweak various settings (hyperparameters) like the fuel mixture, tire pressure, and wing angles to optimize its performance. These two scripts provide different ways to find the best "settings" for your "race car" model.

201

Script 1: Create a new textfile named huggingface_trainer_random_search.py in VS code, command prompt or terminal. - The "Assisted Tuning" Approach

```python
from transformers import Trainer, TrainingArguments
from ray import tune
from transformers import AutoModelForSequenceClassification

training_args = TrainingArguments(
    output_dir="./results",
    evaluation_strategy="epoch",
    save_strategy="epoch",
    learning_rate=2e-5,  # Initial Value
    per_device_train_batch_size=16,  # Initial Value
    per_device_eval_batch_size=64,  # Initial Value
    num_train_epochs=3,
    weight_decay=0.01,
    push_to_hub=False,  # Change to True if deploying to hub
)

def model_init(trial):
    return AutoModelForSequenceClassification.from_pretrained(
        model_checkpoint, num_labels=2
    ).to(training_args.device)

trainer = Trainer(
    model=model,
    args=training_args,
    train_dataset=tokenized_datasets["train"],
    eval_dataset=tokenized_datasets["validation"],
    tokenizer=tokenizer,
    data_collator=data_collator,
)
```

continued on next page..

```python
# Ray Tune Search Space
trainer.hyperparameter_search(
    direction="maximize",
    backend="ray",
    metric="eval_accuracy",
    compute_objective=None,
    n_trials=2,
    stop=None,
    time_budget_s=None,
    resources_per_trial=None,
    local_dir=None,
    name=None,
    loggers=None,
    storage_path=None,
    load_best=False,
    save_trials=False,
    model_init=model_init,
    callbacks=None,
    trial_name_creator=None,
    trial_dirname_creator=None,
    hp_space=lambda trial: {
        "learning_rate": trial.uniform("learning_rate", 2e-5, 5e-5),  # Learning
Rate
        "per_device_train_batch_size":
trial.choice("per_device_train_batch_size", [8, 16, 32]),  # Batch Sizes
        "num_train_epochs": trial.choice("num_train_epochs", [2, 3, 4]),  #
Epochs
        "weight_decay": trial.uniform("weight_decay", 0.0, 0.1),  # Decay
Weights
    }
)
```

203

6.7 Automating Hyperparameter Tuning with Hugging Face's Trainer and Ray Tune

Create a new text file named `huggingface_trainer_random_search`.py in VS Code, command prompt, or terminal. This approach is like having a team of mechanics and computer systems helping you tune a race car.

This script uses powerful tools like Hugging Face's Trainer and Ray Tune to automate the process of finding good hyperparameter settings. It takes your existing machine learning model, defines a range of possible values for different settings (hyperparameters), and then automatically tries out many combinations of those settings, training the model each time to see how well it performs. The script uses random search to explore different settings and record the results for comparison.

This is a good option if you want to leverage powerful, pre-built tools to automate the tuning process and are comfortable working with the Hugging Face Transformers library and Ray Tune.

204

How to Use It (Basic Steps)

1. **Install the Required Libraries.** Ensure you have the necessary libraries installed. Run commands like:

```
pip install transformers
pip install ray[tune]
pip install scikit-learn
```

2. **Adapt the Script to Your Model and Data**

Replace the example placeholders in the code with your actual model, training data, and evaluation data. For instance, specify where the model and data are located.

3. **Define Your Search Space**

4. **Run the Script**

Open a terminal or command prompt, navigate to the directory where you saved the script, and run it:

```
python huggingface_trainer_random_search.py
```

205

By following these steps, you can efficiently tune your model's hyperparameters, leveraging advanced tools to automate the process and achieve optimal performance.

The script uses powerful tools like Hugging Face's Trainer and Ray Tune to automate the process of finding good hyperparameter settings. It takes your existing machine learning model, defines a range of possible values for different settings (hyperparameters), and then automatically tries out many combinations of those settings, training the model each time to see how well it performs. Using random search, it explores different settings and records the results for comparison. This is a good option if you want to leverage powerful, pre-built tools to automate the tuning process and are comfortable working with the Hugging Face Transformers library and Ray Tune.

Script 2: manual_random_search.py - The "Hands-On" Approach

206

This script provides a more basic and manual way to perform random search, giving you more control over the process but requiring more coding. Think of it as manually trying out different settings on the race car yourself.

Here's what the script does: It defines a set of possible values for different hyperparameters. Then, it loops through a specified number of trials, randomly selecting hyperparameter values for each trial, training the model, and evaluating its performance.

```
import random

# Define the hyperparameter search space
learning_rates = [5e-5, 2e-5, 3e-5]
batch_sizes = [16, 32]
num_epochs = [2, 3, 4]

best_accuracy = 0
best_params = {}

for i in range(10):  # Run 10 random trials
    # Randomly sample hyperparameters
    lr = random.choice(learning_rates)
    bs = random.choice(batch_sizes)
    ep = random.choice(num_epochs)

    print(f"Trial {i+1}: lr={lr}, batch_size={bs}, epochs={ep}")

    # Create and train your model with these hyperparameters (replace with your actual model training code)
    model = YourModel(...)  # Instantiate your model
    history = model.train(learning_rate=lr, batch_size=bs, num_epochs=ep, ...) #Train Model

    # Evaluate your model (replace with your actual evaluation code)
    accuracy = model.evaluate(...)#Evaluate

    print(f"  Accuracy: {accuracy}")

    # Keep track of the best results
    if accuracy > best_accuracy:
        best_accuracy = accuracy
        best_params = {"learning_rate": lr, "batch_size": bs, "num_epochs": ep}

print(f"Best Accuracy: {best_accuracy}")
print(f"Best Hyperparameters: {best_params}")
```

When to use it: This approach is good if you want a deeper understanding of the random search process, you want more control over the training and evaluation loops, or you don't want to rely on external libraries like Hugging Face Transformers and Ray Tune.

How to Use It (Basic Steps)

1. **Adapt the script to your model and data:**
   Replace placeholders in the code where it says
   YourModel(...), model.train(...), and
   model.evaluate(...) with your actual code

208

for creating, training, and evaluating your machine learning model.

2. **Define the hyperparameter search space:** Modify the `learning_rates`, `batch_sizes`, and `num_epochs` lists (or create your own lists for other hyperparameters you want to tune).

3. **Run the script:** Open a terminal or command prompt, navigate to the directory where you saved the script, and run it:

```
python manual_random_search.py
```

This script is a template. You must modify it to work with your specific machine learning model and data. You have complete control over the training and evaluation process, but you'll need to write more code than with the Hugging Face Trainer script.

By using this hands-on approach, you can gain a deeper understanding of hyperparameter tuning and have more control over the process, leading to potentially better optimization for your specific needs.

209

General Steps to Get Started

To get started with your machine learning project, follow these general steps:

1. **Choose a Machine Learning Task**: Decide what you want your model to do, such as classify images, translate text, or predict stock prices.

2. **Get a Model**: Use a pre-trained model (transfer learning) or build a model from scratch.

3. **Prepare Your Data**: Clean, preprocess, and split your data into training, validation, and test sets. This is crucial for training your model effectively.

4. **Choose a Script**: Select the script that best suits your needs and skill level. The Hugging Face Trainer is generally easier if you are using Hugging Face models.

5. **Adapt the Script**: Modify the script to work with your model, data, and desired hyperparameters. This is the most important step in the process.

210

6. **Run the Script**: Execute the script to train your model.

7. **Analyze the Results**: Examine which settings (hyperparameters) gave you the best results.

8. **Iterate**: Refine your search space and run the tuning process again to see if you can find even better settings.

Important Considerations

- **Computational Resources**: Hyperparameter tuning can be computationally expensive, especially with large models and datasets. Be prepared for the scripts to take some time to finish running.

- **Overfitting**: Be cautious not to overfit your model to the validation data during hyperparameter tuning. Use a separate test set to evaluate the final performance of your model.

- **Experimentation**: Don't be afraid to experiment with different hyperparameters and search

211

strategies. There's no one-size-fits-all approach to hyperparameter tuning.

6.8 A "Tweak and Test" Approach

The core idea is to experiment rapidly:

- **Start Small**: Tweak one or two settings at a time. Don't try to change everything at once, or you won't know what caused the change in performance.

Use a Small Dataset: Training on the full dataset for every trial can be time-consuming. Test your changes on a small, representative subset of your data to get quick feedback. This allows you to explore the hyperparameter space more efficiently. Imagine you have a pizza with many toppings. When trying different sauce mixes, you would test on smaller slices rather than making a whole new pizza to avoid wasting a lot of food if the sauce combination doesn't taste good.

212

"See What Sticks": The goal is to find hyperparameters that improve performance. If a change doesn't help, revert it and try something else.

By starting with random search and using this "tweak and test" approach, you can quickly gain valuable insights into your model's behavior and find a good set of hyperparameters without spending excessive time and resources. It's a pragmatic and effective way to begin your hyperparameter tuning journey.

6.9 How to Implement Random Search (Simplified Examples)

Using Hugging Face's Trainer provides a convenient way to perform random search. You can specify a search space (a range of values) for the hyperparameters you want to tune, and let the Trainer run multiple training runs with randomly sampled values from that space. This approach automates the process and helps you find the best settings for your model efficiently.

213

Random search is a practical and efficient method for hyperparameter tuning, especially when you have a large search space. Hugging Face's Trainer API streamlines this process by allowing you to specify a hyperparameter search space and automatically run multiple training trials with randomly sampled values.

Here's how to implement random search using Hugging Face's Trainer:

1. Define a Model Initialization Function

You need a model_init function so that the Trainer can reinitialize the model for each trial. This ensures each run starts from the same state.

```python
def model_init(trial):
    from transformers import AutoModelForSequenceClassification
    return AutoModelForSequenceClassification.from_pretrained(
        "bert-base-uncased"
    )
```

214

2. Specify the Hyperparameter Search Space

Define the hyperparameter ranges you want to search. You can use a dictionary where each key is a hyperparameter name and the value is a function that returns a randomly sampled value. For example:

```python
def hp_space(trial):
    return {
        "learning_rate": trial.suggest_float("learning_rate", 1e-5, 5e-3, log=True),
        "num_train_epochs": trial.suggest_int("num_train_epochs", 2, 5),
        "per_device_train_batch_size": trial.suggest_categorical("per_device_train_batch_size", [8, 16, 32]),
    }
```

215

3. Run the Hyperparameter Search

Call the hyperparameter_search() method on your Trainer instance, specifying the search direction (e.g., "maximize" for accuracy), the backend (such as "optuna" or "ray"), and the number of trials.

```python
from transformers import Trainer, TrainingArguments

training_args = TrainingArguments(
    output_dir="./results",
    evaluation_strategy="epoch",
    save_strategy="epoch",
)

trainer = Trainer(
    model_init=model_init,
    args=training_args,
    train_dataset=train_dataset,
    eval_dataset=eval_dataset,
    tokenizer=tokenizer,
)

best_trial = trainer.hyperparameter_search(
    direction="maximize",
    hp_space=hp_space,
    n_trials=10,   # Number of random samples
    backend="optuna",   # Or "ray", "wandb", etc.
)
```

216

4. Review the Results

After the search, best_trial will contain the best hyperparameters found and their corresponding evaluation metric.

Step	Description
Define model_init	Function to reinitialize the model for each trial
Specify hp_space	Function returning a dictionary of hyperparameter sampling strategies
Run hyperparameter_search	Method to execute the random search over the specified number of trials
Review results	Access the best hyperparameters and metrics from the search

This approach automates hyperparameter tuning, enabling efficient exploration of the search space and helping you identify the best settings for your model.

6.10 Memory Management: Making Room to Breathe

Training an LLM is like packing for a trip—those big suitcases (model and data) need to fit in your car (GPU memory). If you overstuff, it won't work. Let's explore ways to lighten the load without losing anything important.

Training LLMs requires significant memory due to their high dimensionality. Efficiently managing memory is

217

key to handling large models without compromising training efficiency. It's like packing a suitcase: you want to fit everything you need without exceeding the weight limit.

Training large language models (LLMs) is like packing a suitcase for a long trip-fitting massive models and datasets into limited GPU memory requires careful planning and smart strategies. Overloading your GPU leads to crashes and inefficiency, so let's explore proven ways to "lighten the load" without sacrificing essential model components.

Key Memory Challenges in LLM Training

- LLMs have billions of parameters, and their memory needs are dominated by model weights, optimizer states, and caches for attention mechanisms

- A single GPU, even with 80 GB of VRAM, often can't accommodate all requirements for large models

218

Strategies to Optimize GPU Memory for LLMs

1. Model and Data Parallelism

- **Model Parallelism:** Split the model across multiple GPUs so each device holds only part of the network. This allows training models larger than a single GPU's memory

- **Data Parallelism:** Each GPU holds a full copy of the model but processes different batches of data. Gradients are synchronized across devices after each step

- Distributed fine-tuning methods can be chosen based on memory estimation tools like LLMem, which predicts peak memory usage and helps select the most efficient approach for your hardware

2. Quantization

- Reduces the precision of model weights (e.g., from 16-bit to 8-bit), shrinking memory

219

requirements with minimal impact on performance

- Useful for both training and inference, especially when hardware is limited.

3. Activation Checkpointing (Recomputation)

- Instead of storing all intermediate activations for backpropagation, only select checkpoints are kept; others are recomputed as needed during the backward pass.

- This trades extra computation for significant memory savings

4. Offloading and Swapping

- Move less frequently used tensors to CPU memory or even NVMe SSDs, freeing up valuable GPU memory for active computations

- Particularly effective for optimizer states and large caches.

220

5. Efficient Attention Mechanisms

- Techniques like **PagedAttention** manage memory for attention caches using virtual memory paging, reducing fragmentation and allowing dynamic allocation

- Systems like **vLLM** and frameworks such as **Jenga** further optimize memory usage by handling non-contiguous storage and flexible caching, enabling larger batches and more concurrent requests

6. Defragmentation and Redundancy Reduction

- Optimize allocation and deallocation patterns to minimize memory fragmentation.

- Reduce duplication of data across processes to maximize available memory

Practical Example: Packing Your LLM Suitcase

221

- **Split the load:** Use model/data parallelism to distribute the model across several GPUs, making the most of available hardware

- **Shrink your items:** Apply quantization and activation checkpointing to reduce the memory footprint of each component

- **Organize smartly:** Use advanced memory management systems (PagedAttention, vLLM, Jenga) to dynamically allocate and reuse memory, minimizing waste and maximizing throughput

- **Offload the extras:** Move infrequently used data to CPU or disk storage, keeping only the essentials in GPU memory

By combining these techniques, you can fit even the largest LLMs into your available hardware "suitcase," ensuring efficient training and inference without overstuffing your GPU.

6.11 Gradient Accumulation: Small Steps, Big Wins

Imagine learning a dance routine. You could practice the whole thing at once (big batch), but if your studio's tiny, you'd practice bits over time instead. Gradient accumulation does that—splitting a big batch into smaller chunks, adding up the lessons (gradients), then updating the model. Same result, less space.

Think of training as learning a language through practice sessions. Instead of waiting for each batch's data, gradient accumulation allows the model to "practice" over multiple batches before updating parameters. This technique reduces memory usage while maintaining stable training progress. It's like learning a language by studying a few words each day, rather than trying to memorize the entire dictionary at once.

Practical Tip: Gradient accumulation is a simple and effective way to reduce memory usage. Experiment with different accumulation steps to find the optimal balance between memory usage and training speed.

223

Training large models on limited hardware is like learning a dance in a small studio: you can't practice the whole routine at once, so you break it into smaller sections and put them together over time. **Gradient accumulation** works the same way for neural networks, allowing you to simulate large batch training even when your GPU memory is limited.

How Gradient Accumulation Works

- Instead of updating model weights after every mini-batch, you accumulate gradients over several mini-batches.

- Only after a set number of accumulation steps do you update the model weights, as if you had processed a much larger batch all at once

- This effectively allows you to train with a large "virtual" batch size, reducing memory requirements since only a small batch is processed at any given time

224

Example

Suppose your GPU can only fit a batch size of 8, but you want the effect of a batch size of 32:

- Set your batch size to 8.

- Set gradient accumulation steps to 4.

- The optimizer will update the weights after 4 mini-batches, using the sum of their gradients, achieving the same effect as a batch size of 32

Why Use Gradient Accumulation?

- **Memory Efficiency:** Only a small batch is loaded into memory at a time, making it possible to train large models or use larger effective batch sizes on limited hardware

- **Stable Training:** Larger effective batch sizes can lead to more stable gradient estimates and smoother training progress

- **Flexible Scaling:** You can adjust the accumulation steps to balance between memory usage and training speed, finding the optimal setup for your hardware and model

Practical Tips

- **Effective Batch Size:** The effective batch size is the product of your per-step batch size and the number of accumulation steps

- **Loss Scaling:** If your loss function averages over the batch, remember to divide the loss by the number of accumulation steps before

226

backpropagation to keep the gradient scale consistent

- **Experiment:** Try different combinations of batch size and accumulation steps to see what works best for your model and hardware.

Summary Table: Batch Size vs. Gradient Accumulation

Per-Step Batch Size	Accumulation Steps	Effective Batch Size	Memory Usage	Update Frequency
32	1	32	High	Every batch
8	4	32	Low	Every 4 batches

Gradient accumulation lets you take "small steps"-processing manageable mini-batches-but still reap the "big wins" of large-batch training, all without overloading your GPU.

227

Code Example (PyTorch):

```
optimizer.zero_grad() # Reset gradients
for i, (inputs, labels) in enumerate(training_set):
    outputs = model(inputs)
    loss = criterion(outputs, labels)
    loss = loss / accumulation_steps # Normalize our loss (if multiple
losses)
    loss.backward() # Calculate Gradients
    if (I+1) % accumulation_steps == 0: # Wait for several backward steps
        optimizer.step() # Now we can do an optimizer step
        optimizer.zero_grad() # Reset gradients
```

This script is part of the process to train a machine learning model using a technique called gradient accumulation. Before starting each training loop, it clears any existing gradient values to ensure that previous calculations don't interfere. The script then processes the training data in batches. For each batch, the model makes predictions, and the loss or error between these predictions and the actual labels is calculated. This loss is normalized and back-propagated to compute gradients. Instead of updating the model's weights immediately after each batch, the gradients are accumulated over several steps. Once the specified number of steps is reached, the accumulated gradients are used to update the model's weights, and the

228

gradients are reset again for the next round. This method allows the model to train effectively without consuming too much memory, making it suitable for large datasets or limited computational resources. In essence, the script ensures efficient training by dividing the process into manageable steps and optimizing memory usage while still improving the model's performance. This method ensures efficient and effective training, especially when dealing with large datasets or limited computational resources. Example: Want a batch of 32 but only fit 8? Set accumulation steps to 4.

6.12 Mixed-Precision Training: Light and Fast

Think of writing a note—big markers take more space than a pencil, but both get the job done. Mixed-precision training uses smaller numbers (16-bit) for most math, switching to bigger ones (32-bit) only when needed. It cuts memory use and speeds things up without messing up accuracy.

Using a combination of lower and higher precision arithmetic (like 16-bit and 32-bit) helps maintain numerical stability without increasing memory consumption. It's like using lighter tools when possible but ensuring they're still effective for the task at hand. It's like switching to a smaller font size to fit more text on a page without losing readability.

Practical Tip: Mixed-precision training can significantly reduce memory usage and speed up training. However, it's important to ensure that your hardware and software support mixed-precision training.

Code Example (PyTorch with Apex):

```
from apex import amp
model, optimizer = amp.initialize(model, optimizer, opt_level="O1")
```

This script is part of the process to train a machine learning model using a technique called gradient accumulation. Before starting each training loop, it clears any existing gradient values to ensure that previous calculations don't interfere. The script then processes the training data in batches. For each batch,

230

the model makes predictions, and the loss or error between these predictions and the actual labels is calculated. This loss is normalized and back-propagated to compute gradients. Instead of updating the model's weights immediately after each batch, the gradients are accumulated over several steps. Once the specified number of steps is reached, the accumulated gradients are used to update the model's weights, and the gradients are reset again for the next round. This method allows the model to train effectively without consuming too much memory, making it suitable for large datasets or limited computational resources. In essence, the script ensures efficient training by dividing the process into manageable steps and optimizing memory usage while still improving the model's performance.

Choosing the right batch size is crucial—it's like adjusting the gear on your bicycle. Smaller batches reduce memory usage but slow down training, while larger batches speed things up but require more

231

memory. Finding the optimal balance ensures efficient use of computational resources.

Practical Tip: Experiment with different batch sizes to find the largest batch size that fits in your GPU memory. If you're running out of memory, try reducing the batch size or using gradient accumulation.

Practical Tip: Test Your Limits Run a small batch (like 4) and check memory use with `nvidia-smi`. If it's tight, lower the batch size or add gradient accumulation. Free tools like Colab Pro can help you experiment without breaking the bank!

6.13 Parallelization: Calling in the Team

Training can feel like cooking a feast solo—overwhelming! Parallelization is like bringing in a team to chop veggies and stir pots at the same time. It significantly accelerates LLM training by leveraging multiple computing resources. Imagine having a team of chefs working together to prepare a large meal, rather than one chef doing everything.

232

Training large language models (LLMs) is like preparing a banquet-doing it alone is slow and overwhelming, but with a team, each person tackles a task and the whole process speeds up. **Parallelization** brings that teamwork to LLM training, distributing the workload across multiple computing resources (GPUs or even machines) to dramatically accelerate the process and enable training at scales that would be impossible for a single device.

Why Parallelization Matters

Speed: Multiple GPUs or nodes work simultaneously, slashing the time needed for training massive models

Scale: Enables training of models and datasets far larger than a single device's memory or compute capacity

Efficiency: Optimizes hardware use and reduces idle time, ensuring every resource contributes to the task

233

Type	How It Works	When to Use	Pros	Cons
Data Parallelism	Full model copy on each GPU; different data batches per GPU; gradients synced	Dataset is huge, model fits on a single GPU	Simple, widely supported, scalable	Duplicates model in memory on each device
Model Parallelism	Model split across GPUs (layers/parameters)	Model too large for a single GPU	Trains very large models	Complex coordination, communication overhead
Pipeline Parallelism	Model divided into sequential stages, each on a different GPU	Model is deep, can be split into stages	Balances memory/compute, high throughput	Pipeline "bubbles" (idle time)
Tensor Parallelism	Individual tensors split across GPUs	Large matrix operations, fine-grained splitting	Fine-grained, efficient for big ops	Complex implementation
Hybrid Parallelism	Mix of above (e.g., data + model)	Very large models, large clusters	Maximizes hardware use	Complex setup and tuning

How These Methods Work Together

Data Parallelism: Each GPU gets a full model copy and a slice of the data. After processing, gradients are averaged and weights are synchronized

- **Model Parallelism**: The model itself is split-each GPU holds only part of the model, letting you train models larger than a single GPU's memory

234

- **Pipeline Parallelism**: The model is divided into stages, and micro-batches of data flow through the pipeline, keeping all GPUs busy

- **Tensor Parallelism**: Large tensors (like weight matrices) are split across GPUs, so each device computes a portion of the operation

- **Hybrid Parallelism**: Combines strategies (e.g., data + model parallelism) for optimal performance on very large clusters or models

Imagine you have a model too big for one GPU and a dataset too large to process quickly:

- **Step 1:** Use model parallelism to split the model across two GPUs.

- **Step 2:** Apply data parallelism so each model split processes a different batch of data on each GPU.

- **Step 3:** If even finer control is needed, use tensor or pipeline parallelism for specific layers or operations.

235

Parallelization is essential for efficient and scalable large language model (LLM) training. The optimal strategy depends on factors such as your model size, dataset, and available hardware. Modern frameworks like PyTorch and TensorFlow, as well as libraries such as Horovod, provide built-in support for these parallelization techniques, making distributed training more accessible than ever. For the largest models and datasets, combining multiple parallelization approaches-known as hybrid parallelism-often yields the best results, maximizing hardware utilization and overall training efficiency.

By "calling in the team" with parallelization, you can train bigger models, faster, and more efficiently-turning an overwhelming solo task into a streamlined, collaborative effort.

6.14 Data Parallelism: Split the Workload

Picture a class splitting a big homework packet—each kid does a page, then they combine answers. Data parallelism splits your data across multiple GPUs, each

236

training a copy of the model on its chunk. They share updates, making it faster than one GPU slogging through alone. Each worker has a copy of the model and trains on different subsets of the data.

A practical tip: Data parallelism is a good starting point for parallelizing LLM training. It's relatively easy to implement and can provide significant speedups.

Code Example (PyTorch with DistributedDataParallel):

```
import torch.distributed as dist
dist.init_process_group(backend="nccl")
model = DistributedDataParallel(model, device_ids=[dist.get_rank()])
```

This script is designed to train a machine learning model using multiple GPUs or computers. It starts by importing the PyTorch library for distributed training and initializing a group of processes to communicate with each other. The script then wraps the model in a special class that ensures the model's parameters are synchronized across all the devices being used.

237

This setup allows the model to be trained faster and more efficiently by spreading the workload across multiple GPUs or computers. It enables handling larger models and datasets that a single GPU or computer might not be able to manage alone.

In essence, the script sets up a collaborative training environment, making use of multiple resources to speed up the training process and handle larger data loads.

Data parallelism is like assigning different sections of a large homework packet to students in a class: each GPU processes a subset of the data, trains a full model copy, and synchronizes updates to accelerate training. This approach is ideal when your model fits on a single GPU but your dataset is too large or training is too slow.

How Data Parallelism Works

- **Split the data:** The dataset is divided into smaller batches, with each GPU processing a unique subset.

238

- **Replicate the model:** Each GPU holds an identical copy of the model and optimizer.

- **Synchronize gradients:** After each backward pass, gradients are averaged across all GPUs using collective communication (e.g., `all-reduce`).

- **Update weights:** All model copies stay in sync by applying the averaged gradients.

Key Advantages

- **Speed:** Training time scales inversely with the number of GPUs (e.g., 4 GPUs = 4x faster).

- **Simplicity:** PyTorch's `DistributedDataParallel` (DDP) automates gradient synchronization.

- **Scalability:** Works seamlessly across multiple machines (nodes) for large clusters.

6.15 Implementation Steps (PyTorch DDP)

1. Initialize the Distributed Environment

239

```python
import torch
import torch.distributed as dist
from torch.nn.parallel import import DistributedDataParallel as DDP

def setup(rank, world_size):
    dist.init_process_group(
        backend="nccl",  # Optimized for NVIDIA GPUs
        init_method="env://",
        rank=rank,
        world_size=world_size
    )
    torch.cuda.set_device(rank)
```

240

2. Wrap the Model with DDP

```python
def train(rank, world_size):
    setup(rank, world_size)

    # Model setup
    model = MyModel().to(rank)
    ddp_model = DDP(model, device_ids=[rank])

    # Optimizer and loss function
    optimizer = torch.optim.Adam(ddp_model.parameters())
    loss_fn = torch.nn.CrossEntropyLoss()

    # Data loader (sharded per GPU)
    train_loader = get_distributed_dataloader(batch_size=32, rank=rank)

    # Training loop
    for batch in train_loader:
        inputs, labels = batch
        outputs = ddp_model(inputs.to(rank))
        loss = loss_fn(outputs, labels.to(rank))
        loss.backward()
        optimizer.step()
        optimizer.zero_grad()
```

3. Launch Training with `torchrun`

```bash
# Launch on 4 GPUs
torchrun --nproc_per_node=4 --nnodes=1 train_script.py
```

Practical Considerations

241

- **Batch Size:** The effective batch size is `per_gpu_batch_size * num_gpus`. Adjust learning rates accordingly.

- **Data Sharding:** Use `DistributedSampler` to ensure each GPU gets unique data slices.

- **Mixed Precision:** Combine with `torch.cuda.amp` for memory savings and speed

When to use Data Parallelism

Scenario	Solution
Model fits on one GPU	Data parallelism
Model too large for one GPU	Hybrid (data + model parallelism)
Extremely large datasets	Multi-node data parallelism

Performance Tips

- **Use NCCL Backend:** Ensures fast GPU-to-GPU communication

- **Avoid CPU Offloading:** Keep data and models on GPUs to minimize transfer overhead.

242

- **Profile Communication:** Tools like PyTorch Profiler help identify bottlenecks

Data parallelism is the "gateway" technique for distributed LLM training, offering a straightforward path to faster iterations. By splitting the workload across GPUs and automating synchronization, it lets you focus on model design rather than infrastructure.

6.16 In PyTorch, it's a breeze with DataParallel:

Model Parallelism: Divide the Model

Now imagine a huge recipe book too big for one chef. Model parallelism splits the model across GPUs—one handles the first layers, another the rest. It's trickier but perfect for giant LLMs that won't fit on one card.

Think of distributing tasks among workers in a library— each worker handles part of the books. Model parallelism distributes model components across workers to process data efficiently without overwhelming individual resources. Each worker has a

243

different part of the model, and they work together to process the data.

Practical Tip: Start with Data

Got multiple GPUs? Try data parallelism first—it's simpler. Use cloud services like AWS or Google Cloud if you're short on hardware—just rent a multi-GPU setup for a test run!

When training massive LLMs that don't fit on a single GPU, model parallelism acts like splitting a giant recipe book among chefs-each GPU handles a portion of the model's layers. While trickier than data parallelism, this approach enables training models that would otherwise be impossible due to hardware constraints.

How Model Parallelism Works

- **Split the model:** Assign specific layers or components to different GPUs (e.g., first 10 layers on GPU 0, remaining layers on GPU 1).

244

- **Sequential processing:** Data flows through GPUs in sequence, with intermediate outputs transferred between devices.

- **Manual configuration:** Unlike data parallelism, you must explicitly define how the model is divided across GPUs.

Example: Splitting a Model in PyTorch

```python
import torch.nn as nn

class SplitModel(nn.Module):
    def __init__(self):
        super().__init__()
        self.layer1 = nn.Linear(1024, 2048).to('cuda:0')  # First GPU
        self.layer2 = nn.Linear(2048, 4096).to('cuda:1')  # Second GPU

    def forward(self, x):
        x = self.layer1(x.to('cuda:0'))  # Move input to GPU 0
        x = self.layer2(x.to('cuda:1'))  # Move output to GPU 1
        return x
```

245

When to Use Model Parallelism

Scenario	Solution
Model exceeds GPU memory	Model parallelism
Extremely large layers	Tensor parallelism
Hybrid needs	Combine with data parallelism

6.17 Model Parallelism vs. Data Parallelism

Category	Data Parallelism	Model Parallelism
Use Case	Large datasets, small models	Models too large for one GPU
Ease of Use	Simple (automatic splitting)	Complex (manual layer assignment)
Memory Usage	Duplicates model on all GPUs	Splits model across GPUs
Communication	Synchronizes gradients	Transfers intermediate activations
Scalability	Limited by model size	Limited by layer dependencies

Model Parallelism Practical Tips

1. **Start with Data Parallelism:** If your model fits on one GPU, use `DataParallel` or `DistributedDataParallel` for easier scaling.

246

```python
python
model = nn.DataParallel(model).to(device)   # Single-line implementation
```

- **Leverage Cloud GPUs:** Rent multi-GPU instances on platforms like:

- **AWS:** p4d.24xlarge instances with 8x A100 GPUs

Google Cloud: Create GPU clusters with pre-configured PyTorch environments

```bash
bash
gcloud compute instances create $INSTANCE_NAME \
  --accelerator="type=nvidia-tesla-v100,count=4" \
  --image-family="pytorch-latest-gpu"
```

Combine Strategies: For massive models, use hybrid parallelism:

- Split the model across GPUs (model parallelism)

- Distribute data batches (data parallelism)

247

Key Challenges

- **Manual Optimization:** Requires careful balancing of computational load between GPUs.

- **Communication Overhead:** Frequent data transfers between devices can bottleneck performance.

- **Debugging Complexity:** Errors often manifest differently across devices.

Model parallelism unlocks training of cutting-edge LLMs but demands careful planning. By strategically dividing layers across GPUs and leveraging cloud scalability, you can tackle even the largest models without hardware limitations.

Advanced Optimization Methods: Smoothing the Ride

Optimization methods are like GPS for your model— helping it find the fastest route to learning. Basic ones like SGD (stochastic gradient descent) work, but these advanced tricks make it smoother and quicker. Modern

248

optimization methods enhance the training process by making adjustments that improve learning efficiency.

6.18 Adam: The Adaptive Star

Think of a student tweaking study time based on what's tough—more on math, less on spelling. Adam (Adaptive Moment Estimation) adjusts learning rates for each part of the model using past progress, making updates fast and steady. It's a favorite for LLMs! Picture a student adjusting their study habits based on recent progress reports to optimize exam preparation. Adam adapts learning rates across parameters using estimates of first and second moments, providing efficient and robust parameter updates.

Adam (**Adaptive Moment Estimation)** is the optimizer of choice for training large language models (LLMs) and deep neural networks, thanks to its ability to dynamically adjust learning rates for each model parameter based on past training progress. Imagine a student who studies more on subjects where they're struggling and less on those they've mastered-Adam

249

brings this adaptive, personalized approach to machine learning optimization.

How Adam Works

Adam combines two key concepts:

- **Momentum:** Keeps track of the direction and speed of past gradients, smoothing out noisy updates (like a student remembering which topics tripped them up before).

- **Adaptive Learning Rates:** Adjusts the learning rate for each parameter individually, based on the historical average of both the gradients (first moment) and their squares (second moment)

The Algorithm in Brief

1. **First Moment Estimate (Mean):** Tracks the average of past gradients.

2. **Second Moment Estimate (Variance):** Tracks the average of the squared gradients.

250

3. **Bias Correction:** Adjusts the moment estimates to counteract their initial bias toward zero.

4. **Parameter Update:** Each parameter gets its own learning rate, scaled by these moment estimates, leading to efficient and stable updates

Why Adam Is a Favorite for LLMs

- **Fast Convergence:** Adam's adaptive nature helps models reach good solutions quickly, speeding up training and reducing compute costs

- **Robustness:** Handles noisy or sparse gradients well, making it ideal for real-world data and massive, complex models like LLMs

- **Minimal Tuning Required:** Default hyperparameters (learning rate = 0.001, $\beta1=0.9$, $\beta2=0.999$) work well in most cases, saving time on manual tuning

- **Widely Supported:** Built into all major ML frameworks (PyTorch, TensorFlow, Keras), making it easy to implement

251

Adam in Practice

- **Parameter Adaptation:** Each parameter's learning rate is tailored to its own learning history, allowing the optimizer to efficiently navigate complex loss landscapes

- **Efficient for Large Models:** Adam's computational and memory efficiency make it suitable for large-scale training, though for extremely large models, memory-optimized variants like Adam-mini are emerging

Key Configuration Parameters

- **Learning Rate (alpha):** Step size for updates (default: 0.001).

- **Beta1:** Decay rate for the first moment (default: 0.9).

- **Beta2:** Decay rate for the second moment (default: 0.999).

- **Epsilon:** Small constant to prevent division by zero (default: 1e-8)

Adam is like a smart, adaptive student-constantly adjusting its study plan based on performance. By adapting learning rates for each parameter using momentum and variance, Adam delivers fast, robust, and efficient training for deep neural networks, making it a star optimizer for LLMs and beyond

6.19 How RMSprop Works

RMSprop (Root Mean Square Propagation) is an adaptive learning rate optimizer that helps your model take smooth, steady steps toward optimal performance-much like pacing yourself in a long race to avoid burning out or lagging behind. By dynamically scaling the learning rate for each parameter based on recent gradient activity, RMSprop ensures stable and efficient convergence, especially in deep learning scenarios.

253

- **Moving Average of Squared Gradients:** RMSprop keeps a running average of the squared gradients for each parameter. This moving average acts as a memory of recent gradient magnitudes, smoothing out the learning process

- **Adaptive Learning Rate:** The optimizer divides the learning rate by the square root of this moving average (plus a small epsilon for stability), allowing each parameter to adapt its update size according to its own learning history

- **Stable Convergence:** By normalizing updates, RMSprop prevents wild swings in parameter values, making learning more stable and reliable, especially when gradients vary widely across layers or over time

RMSprop Update Rule (Simplified)

$$v_t = \beta v_{t-1} + (1 - \beta)g_t^2$$

$$\theta_{t+1} = \theta_t - \frac{\eta}{\sqrt{v_t} + \epsilon}g_t$$

- v_t: Moving average of squared gradients

- β: Decay rate (commonly 0.9)

- g_t: Current gradient

- η: Learning rate

- ϵ: Small constant for numerical stability

Advantages of RMSprop

- **Rapid Convergence:** Often finds optimal solutions faster than vanilla SGD, especially for complex or non-stationary problems

- **Stable Learning:** Smooths out erratic updates, making it easier to train deep or recurrent neural networks

- **Minimal Tuning:** Fewer hyperparameters to adjust, and defaults usually work well

- **Effective for Non-Convex Problems:** Excels in deep learning tasks where loss surfaces are highly irregular

Second-Order Methods: The Fancy Move

Second-order optimization methods, like Newton's Method or L-BFGS, are akin to a pro cyclist fine-tuning gears based on the road ahead. They use not only gradient information but also curvature (the Hessian matrix) to make smarter, more informed parameter updates

. This can lead to faster and more precise convergence, especially for smaller or highly complex problems.

- **Pros:** Superior convergence rates, can escape problematic regions in the loss landscape, and may generalize better in some scenarios

- **Cons:** Computationally expensive and memory-intensive, making them impractical for massive neural networks or LLMs

Practical Tip: Stick with Adam

For most deep learning tasks-especially for beginners or when training LLMs-Adam remains the go-to optimizer. It combines the best of RMSprop and momentum, is robust, and requires little tuning. Start by experimenting with learning rates in the range of $1×10−51×10−5$ to $5×10−55×10−5$ and watch your model improve rapidly

6.20 Your LLM, Optimized and Awesome

With optimizers like RMSprop and Adam, you have powerful tools for efficient, stable, and effective training. These methods-along with smart memory management, parallelization, and careful hyperparameter tuning-help you train better models, faster, and with less hassle. Start small, experiment with settings, and gradually build your expertise. Every tweak brings you closer to LLM mastery-so dive in and let your models shine!

Summary Table: Optimizer Comparison

Optimizer	Adaptive LR	Momentum	Curvature Info	Best For	Complexity
SGD	No	Optional	No	Simple tasks, baseline	Low
RMSprop	Yes	No	No	Deep nets, RNNs, non-stationary	Low
Adam	Yes	Yes	No	LLMs, deep nets, most scenarios	Low
Second-Order	Yes	Yes	Yes	Small/complex models, fine-tuning	High

258

CHAPTER 7: Physical Considerations for LLM Training Systems: Building Your AI Fortress

The Unsung Heroes of LLM Training

Hey, welcome back to LLM - Deep Dive! We've journeyed through code, data, and optimization tricks, but now it's time to talk about something just as crucial: the physical setup that powers your large language model (LLM) training. Think of it like setting up a cozy home for your AI—without a sturdy roof, reliable power, and a cool vibe, your model might not thrive.

The physical stuff—servers, cooling, power, and more—isn't just techy background noise. It's the backbone that keeps your training fast, stable, and affordable. Mess it up, and you're looking at overheated GPUs or crashed runs. This chapter explores the key pieces of this fortress: servers, cooling and power, networking, and a safety net with data management. I'll break it down with simple examples (think baking or road trips!) and tips you can use, whether you're tinkering at home or

259

dreaming big. Ready to roll up your sleeves and build something solid? Let's get to it!

7.1 Server Specifications: The Brain Behind the Operation – Choosing Your Warriors

Your servers are the stars of the show—the brain that powers your LLM's learning. These aren't your everyday computers; they're built to chew through massive data and tough math like champs. At the heart of any LLM training setup is the server—a powerful machine designed to handle the heaviest computational tasks. These servers are equipped with multiple GPUs and CPUs working in concert to process vast amounts of data and train complex models. It's like choosing the right warriors for your army: you need strength, speed, and reliability.

7.2 What Makes a Server Tick?

GPUs are the muscle! NVIDIA GPUs speed up training with tensor cores—think of them as turbo boosters for number-crunching. More GPUs mean quicker results.

260

GPUs are heavy lifters with turbo boosters for number crunching, helping you to speed up training.

CPUs are the manager—handling lighter tasks like shuffling data while GPUs flex. A multi-core CPU keeps things smooth. CPUs help with lighter tasks whilst the GPUs complete more rigorous training.

RAM is short-term memory—128GB or more lets your server juggle big datasets without hiccups. RAM is a server's short-term memory that helps juggle big datasets.

Storage, such as fast SSDs, grabs data in a snap, so your model isn't waiting around. SSDs help to quickly grab data.

Key Considerations:

GPU Density: How many GPUs can the server accommodate? More GPUs generally mean faster training times, but also higher power consumption and cooling requirements.

261

- CPU Cores: While GPUs do the heavy lifting, CPUs are still important for managing the system and handling data preprocessing.

- RAM: Sufficient RAM is crucial for loading and processing large datasets.

- Storage: Fast storage (SSDs or NVMe drives) is essential for quickly loading data during training.

7.3 Big Players in Action

OpenAI's GPT-3 trained on 40 nodes—mini-server hubs —across three data centers, each packed with GPUs. That's how they tackled petabytes of text! NVIDIA's AI labs go even bigger, linking thousands of GPUs for lightning-fast training. It has been reported that OpenAI's GPT-3, which required a massive 40 nodes across three data centers, and NVIDIA's AI research labs have developed custom systems with thousands of GPUs connected via high-speed networks, facilitating faster and more efficient training.

When choosing servers, consider the trade-offs between cost, performance, and scalability. If you're starting small, a single server with multiple GPUs might be sufficient. As your project grows, you can scale up to a multi-server cluster. Consult with hardware vendors and system integrators to get recommendations for servers that are specifically designed for LLM training.

Practical Tip: Start Where You Are

No mega-budget? A single PC with 2-4 GPUs can kick things off. Check out Google Colab's free GPUs for a no-cost test run!

- Rack Mounting: Ensure servers are mounted in standard 19" racks with proper spacing to allow for airflow. Leave enough room in the rack for switches, power distribution units, and cable management.

- Cable Management: Properly label and organize cables to ensure easy maintenance and troubleshooting. Use cable ties or Velcro straps

263

to bundle cables together and keep them out of the way of airflow.

By considering these factors, you can select the right servers to power your LLM training, ensuring strength, speed, and reliability for your computational tasks.

7.4 Cooling and Power Management: Keeping the Heat Off – Preventing Meltdowns

Training an LLM is like revving a race car—it guzzles power and gets hot. Without good cooling and a steady power flow, your setup could stall or fry mid-race. To prevent overheating or power outages, these systems are equipped with robust cooling solutions. It's like ensuring your car engine doesn't overheat during a long race.

7.5 Cooling: Chill Out

Air Cooling uses fans to blow heat away—like opening a window on a hot day. It's cheap and easy for small setups.

264

Liquid Cooling uses coolant pipes to whisk heat off GPUs—think of a car's radiator.

Immersion Cooling involves dunking servers in special fluid—super cool (literally!) but fancy and rare.

Key Considerations:

- Cooling Capacity: How much heat can the cooling system dissipate?

- Power Efficiency: How efficiently does the power supply convert electricity into usable power?

- Redundancy: Are there backup power systems in place to prevent downtime in case of a power outage?

7.6 Cooling Systems:

Air Cooling is the most common and least expensive option. It involves using fans and heatsinks to dissipate heat. A practical tip is to optimize airflow by arranging servers in rows with hot and cold aisles.

265

Liquid Cooling is more efficient than air cooling, but also more expensive and complex. It involves using liquid coolants to transfer heat away from the components. Consider liquid cooling for high-density GPU deployments or in environments where noise is a concern.

Immersion Cooling is the most efficient cooling solution, but also the most expensive and complex. It involves submerging the components in a dielectric fluid. Immersion cooling is ideal for very high-density GPU deployments and can significantly reduce energy consumption.

7.7 Power: Stay Charged

Top-notch power supply units (PSUs) deliver steady juice. Google and Meta run data centers with backup PSUs, ensuring no blackouts.

Choose PSUs with high certifications for maximum efficiency.

266

Practical Tips:

- Monitor the temperature of your components and the ambient temperature of the server room.

- Use a power meter to track the power consumption of your training system.

- Consider using a power distribution unit (PDU) with individual outlet monitoring to track the power consumption of each component in your system.

7.8 Heat Monitoring

Install temperature sensors throughout the server room to monitor heat levels. Use software to alert you if temperatures exceed safe limits.

Fire Suppression

Equip the server room with a fire suppression system suitable for electronic equipment. Avoid water-based systems due to the risk of electrical damage.

267

Practical Tip: Keep an Eye on It

Grab a thermometer for your setup. Use tools to check GPU temps—aim below recommended levels.

By considering these factors and implementing robust cooling and power management solutions, you can keep your training setup running smoothly and prevent any meltdowns.

7.9 Networking: The Highway to Data – Keeping the Data Flowing

When your LLM trains across multiple machines, they need fast roads to share data—and a backup plan if something breaks. Networking and redundancy are your highways and seatbelts. In distributed training setups, where models are trained across multiple GPUs or nodes, efficient interconnectivity is key.

Networking: Speedy Data Lanes

Ethernet is like a basic road—works for small setups, such as linking two PCs.

268

InfiniBand is a high-speed freeway—low lag, huge bandwidth.

NVLink is NVIDIA's express lane—GPUs chat directly, skipping traffic.

Key Considerations:

- Bandwidth: How much data can be transferred per unit of time?

- Latency: How long does it take for data to travel from one node to another?

- Topology: How are the nodes connected to each other?

7.10 Networking Technologies:

Ethernet is a common networking technology that is suitable for smaller clusters. A practical tip is to use fast Ethernet for LLM training.

InfiniBand is a high-performance networking technology that is designed for high-bandwidth, low-latency communication. It is ideal for large-scale distributed training.

NVLink is a high-speed interconnect technology developed by NVIDIA that allows GPUs to communicate directly with each other. NVLink can significantly improve performance for model parallelism.

Choose a networking technology that is appropriate for the size and complexity of your cluster. Optimize your network configuration to minimize latency and maximize bandwidth. Use monitoring tools to track network performance and identify potential bottlenecks.

Test the Connection

Got two machines? Hook them up with a good Ethernet cable. For redundancy, copy your data weekly—easy insurance!

270

7.11 Redundancy: The Safety Net – Protecting Against the Inevitable

To avoid any downtime during training, redundancy is crucial. It's like having a spare tire for your car: you hope you never need it, but you're glad it's there.

Redundancy: Plan B

Power: Dual PSUs (Power Supply Units) mean that if one fails, the other kicks in. This ensures a continuous power supply to your servers without interruption.

Network: Having extra cables or switches keeps your network connections alive, even if one fails. This redundancy ensures that your data flow remains uninterrupted.

Storage: Backups save your data if a drive crashes. By having redundant storage systems, you can protect against data loss and ensure that your data is always available.

271

Key Components to Redundancy

Power Supplies: Equip all servers with redundant power supplies to prevent downtime in case of a power supply failure. Use PSUs with "hot-swap" capabilities for maximum efficiency.

Network Connections: Use redundant network connections to prevent downtime in case of a network failure. Aggregating network links can increase capacity and provide a more reliable connection.

Storage Systems: Implement redundant storage systems to protect against data loss. Use RAID configurations or distributed file systems to ensure data availability and safeguard your valuable information.

By incorporating these redundancy measures, you can create a robust training environment that is resilient to failures and ensures continuous operation, protecting your LLM training process against any inevitable issues.

272

7.12 Data Management: Taming Gigantic Datasets – Keeping Things Organized

Your LLM needs a ton of data—like a giant library—and a comfy server room to thrive. These pieces keep everything organized and running smoothly. Handling massive datasets requires efficient data management systems. It's like having a well-organized library: you need to be able to find the books you need quickly and easily.

Training a large language model (LLM) is like managing a vast, ever-growing library. Success depends not just on having a huge collection of books (data), but on keeping everything organized, accessible, and high-quality. Efficient data management ensures your LLM can learn from massive datasets without getting lost in the clutter.

Why Data Management Matters for LLMs

- **Performance:** The quality, diversity, and cleanliness of your dataset directly affect your model's accuracy and generalization abilities

273

- **Efficiency:** Well-organized data pipelines speed up training and reduce wasted compute resources

- **Compliance and Security:** Sensitive data must be handled carefully to meet privacy regulations and avoid leaks

- **Scalability:** As datasets grow to terabytes or petabytes, robust management systems are essential for smooth scaling

Key Elements of LLM Data Management

1. Data Collection and Curation

- Gather data from diverse, relevant sources (e.g., Common Crawl, Wikipedia, domain-specific corpora)

- Curate for quality, removing duplicates, spam, and irrelevant content to prevent bias and overfitting.

2. Preprocessing and Annotation

274

- Clean, tokenize, and format text for model consumption.

- Annotate data for supervised tasks, using automated or manual labeling tools to ensure accuracy and consistency

3. Deduplication and Filtering

- Remove duplicate documents and filter out low-quality or harmful content.

- Use automated tools and rule-based systems for scalable, consistent filtering

4. Data Storage and Access

- Store data efficiently using distributed file systems or cloud storage.

- Ensure fast, reliable access for training pipelines, with robust backup and versioning.

5. Data Management Systems

275

- Employ integrated platforms (like Data-Juicer or Oasis) to automate curation, filtering, deduplication, and assessment

- Modular systems allow for zero-code or low-code customization, making it easier to adapt to evolving needs

6. Monitoring and Feedback

- Continuously monitor data quality and model performance.

- Implement feedback loops to refine datasets and address issues as they arise

Popular Open-Source Datasets for LLMs

- **Common Crawl:** Billions of web pages, updated monthly.

- **RefinedWeb:** Deduplicated, filtered version of Common Crawl.

- **The Pile:** 800 GB from 22 diverse sources.

276

- **C4:** Cleaned English web data.

- **Wikipedia, BookCorpus, ROOTS:** High-quality, curated text corpora for general and multilingual training

Challenges in LLM Data Management

- **Data Scarcity in Niche Domains:** Can lead to imbalanced training and poor generalization

- **Annotation Costs and Errors:** Manual labeling is expensive and error-prone; automation helps but isn't perfect

- **Security and Privacy:** Protecting sensitive information is critical

- **Scalability:** Handling, processing, and storing tens of terabytes or more requires robust infrastructure

Practical Tips for Organizing LLM Data

277

- **Automate where possible:** Use data management platforms to streamline curation, annotation, and filtering.

- **Version control your datasets:** Track changes and enable reproducibility.

- **Monitor data quality:** Regularly assess for bias, duplication, and relevance.

- **Document your data pipeline:** Keep clear records of sources, processing steps, and curation decisions.

A well-organized data management system is the backbone of any successful LLM project. By treating your dataset like a carefully maintained library, you ensure your model has the best possible foundation for learning, scaling, and delivering accurate results.

7.13 Data Management: Taming the Beast

LLMs munch on huge datasets. Hadoop HDFS splits data across servers, making it fast and safe. Cloud options like AWS S3 work too—scalable and simple.

278

Key Considerations:

- **Storage Capacity**: How much data can the system store?

  Can the system scale to petabytes as your dataset grows? Solutions like Hadoop HDFS and cloud object storage are built to expand easily by adding more nodes or storage buckets.

- **Data Access Speed**: How quickly can the data be accessed?

  How quickly can your training pipeline read and write data? Distributed systems like HDFS split files into blocks and store them across multiple nodes, enabling parallel access and high throughput- essential for big data analytics and LLM training.

- **Data Integrity**: How can you ensure that the data is accurate and consistent?

  Is your data accurate, consistent, and protected from loss? HDFS ensures this through replication (default: three copies per block), automatic failure recovery, and self-healing features. Cloud storage providers offer built-in redundancy and strong consistency models.

279

Data Management Systems:

Hadoop Distributed File System (HDFS) is a distributed file system that is designed for storing and processing large datasets. It's a good choice for storing and managing large datasets used for LLM training.

Hadoop Distributed File System (HDFS)

- **Distributed Architecture:**
  Splits files into blocks and distributes them across many nodes, allowing for massive scale and fault tolerance

- **Fault Tolerance:**
  Replicates data blocks across nodes; if one node fails, data remains available from replicas. The system automatically re-replicates lost blocks to maintain redundancy

- **Cost Effective:**
  Runs on commodity hardware, making it an affordable choice for storing huge datasets

280

- **Integration:**

  Works seamlessly with analytics tools like Hive, Pig, and Spark, enabling efficient data processing for LLM training

- **Security:**

  Supports authentication (e.g., Kerberos) and fine-grained access control for data protection

Object Storage is a scalable and cost-effective storage solution that is ideal for storing unstructured data. It's a good choice for storing data that is not frequently accessed.

Data Backup

Implement automated data backup procedures to protect against data loss. Use a combination of on-site and off-site backups to ensure data can be recovered in the event of a disaster.

Archiving

281

Archive older or less frequently used data to free up storage space on primary systems. Ensure archived data can be easily restored when needed.

By setting up efficient data management systems, you can keep your gigantic datasets organized, accessible, and safe, ensuring smooth and effective training for your LLM.

7.14 Server Room Layout: A Well-Laid-Out Environment – Designing for Efficiency

Designing a server room is much like planning a high-performance kitchen-everything needs its place, airflow must be optimized, and the environment should be safe, accessible, and ergonomic. A well-designed server room not only boosts efficiency but also extends the life of your equipment and reduces downtime.

Core Principles for Server Room Layout

Airflow Management

- **Hot and Cold Aisles:** Arrange server racks in alternating rows so that cold air intakes face each other (cold aisle) and hot air exhausts face each other (hot aisle). This setup ensures cold air is drawn into the front of the servers and hot air is expelled out the back, preventing recirculation and overheating

- **Containment Systems:** Use aisle containment (hot or cold) to further isolate and direct airflow, maximizing cooling efficiency and minimizing energy waste

- **Raised Floors and Perforated Tiles:** Raised floors allow cool air to be distributed evenly through perforated tiles, targeting critical areas and improving temperature regulation

- **Seal Air Gaps:** Use blanking panels and brush grommets to seal gaps in racks and cable openings, preventing air leaks and mixing of hot and cold air

Accessibility

283

- **Space for Maintenance:** Leave enough clearance around racks (at least 36 inches in front and back) for easy access to cables, components, and equipment. This minimizes disruptions during upgrades or repairs

- **Organized Layout:** Use 4-post racks for stability and plan for future expansion. Ensure the room is large enough for current and anticipated equipment

- **Cable Management:** Employ cable trays, vertical and horizontal cable managers, and clearly labeled pathways to avoid clutter and accidental disconnections

Safety and Environmental Controls

- **Clean and Dust-Free:** Keep the environment clean and dust-free to prevent overheating and hardware failures. Avoid placing equipment on unstable surfaces

284

- **Redundant Power:** Use uninterruptible power supplies (UPS) and power distribution units (PDUs) to protect against power outages and surges

- **Environmental Monitoring:** Install sensors to track temperature, humidity, and power usage. Set up alerts for anomalies, enabling quick response to potential issues

- **Fire Safety:** Integrate smoke detection and suppression systems for added protection

Layout Best Practices

Best Practice	Description
Hot/Cold Aisle Layout	Arrange racks for optimal airflow and cooling efficiency.
Raised Floors	Provide space for cables and direct cool air where needed.
Cable Management	Prevent clutter and ensure easy access with trays and organizers.
Redundant Power	Use UPS and PDUs for continuous, safe operation.
Environmental Monitoring	Track temperature, humidity, and power for early issue detection.
Clean, Open Space	Maintain cleanliness and allow room for both airflow and maintenance.
Ergonomic Workspaces	Provide comfortable, well-lit areas for IT staff to work.

Tips for Home or Small Setups

- Place your PC or server on a sturdy desk with space around it.

- Use a fan for basic airflow if no dedicated cooling is available.

- Keep the area clean and avoid stacking items on or around your equipment.

- Back up data regularly, even to simple external drives.

A well-laid-out server room is the foundation of efficient, reliable IT operations. By prioritizing airflow, accessibility, safety, and organization, you ensure your servers run smoothly, stay cool, and are easy to maintain-just like a well-designed kitchen makes every meal easier to prepare.

7.15 Building the Foundation for LLM Success

And that's a wrap on Chapter 7! The physical side of LLM training—servers, cooling, power, networking,

286

redundancy, and layout—is your fortress's foundation. From setting up your tools to designing the model, feeding it data, and fine-tuning the results, you've got the basics to make something amazing. It's not just about tech specs; it's about crafting a reliable home for your AI.

You don't need a tech empire to start—a single GPU rig with a fan and a backup drive gets you in the game. As you grow, cloud services or bigger setups can level you up. Every step—whether it's tweaking a cable or checking the temp—makes your LLM stronger. So, grab your gear, set up your space, and let's train something incredible. Your AI fortress is ready to rock!

In conclusion, the physical infrastructure of LLM training systems is a complex interplay of powerful hardware, efficient cooling, robust power management, high-speed networking, redundancy, and strategic data handling. By carefully considering each component, these systems can efficiently train models to understand and generate human-like text, paving the way for a future where AI enhances our daily lives. This is not just about tech specs; it's about creating a stable, reliable, and scalable environment that can support your LLM training journey.

CHAPTER 8: Best Practices for Managing Large Language Model Training Projects: Steering Your LLM to Success

Navigating the LLM Training Maze

Hey there, welcome to Chapter 8 of LLM - Deep Dive! We've tackled hardware, software, data, and training tricks, but now it's time to zoom out and talk about keeping it all together. Training a large language model (LLM) is a big adventure, and without a solid plan, it's easy to get lost in the maze of code, data, and teamwork. That's where this chapter comes in—your friendly guide to managing LLM projects like a pro.

Think of this as your project playbook. Whether you're flying solo or working with a crew, good organization and collaboration can make or break your success. We'll cover version control to track changes, documentation to keep things clear, knowledge sharing to spark ideas, and communication to keep everyone in sync. I'll break it down with simple examples—like

289

baking or road trips—and toss in tips you can use right away, even if you're just starting out. Ready to steer your LLM to greatness? Let's dive in!

8.1 Version Control: Your Code's Time Machine

Imagine you're baking a cake and wish you could rewind time to fix a recipe mistake or try a new twist without losing your original. That's the magic of **version control** for your code-it's a time machine that lets you track every change, undo errors, experiment freely, and collaborate with others without descending into chaos.

What Is Version Control?

Version control systems (VCS) are essential tools that track and record every change made to your codebase, providing a robust framework for managing software development. With a VCS, you can easily rewind to any previous version of your code, branch off to experiment with new ideas without affecting the main project, merge different contributions smoothly, and track exactly who made changes, when, and why.

290

Version control is crucial for several reasons. It enables mistake recovery, allowing you to undo bugs or accidental deletions by reverting to earlier versions. It supports safe experimentation, as you can test new features or ideas in isolated branches without risking the stability of the main project. Collaboration becomes seamless, with multiple people able to work on the same codebase and merge their work efficiently. Additionally, every change is documented with a message, creating a living history of your project, and the system provides auditability by making it easy to review and compare changes over time.

Among version control tools, Git is the most widely used due to its speed, distributed nature, and flexibility. Online platforms such as GitHub, GitLab, and Bitbucket host Git repositories and offer additional features like pull requests, issue tracking, code reviews, and continuous integration/continuous deployment (CI/CD) integration, making them indispensable for modern software development teams.

291

Typical Workflow with Git

1. **Initialize a Repository:**

```bash
git init
```

- **Track Changes:**

```bash
git add filename.py
git commit -m "Add new feature"
```

- **Branch and Merge:**

```bash
git branch new-idea
git checkout new-idea
# Make changes
git commit -am "Try new approach"
git checkout main
git merge new-idea
```

292

- **Collaborate Remotely:**

```bash
git push origin main
git pull origin main
```

Best Practices

- **Commit Often:** Save your work regularly with clear messages.

- **Branch for Features:** Use branches for new features, bug fixes, or experiments.

- **Review Before Merging:** Use pull requests and code reviews to maintain quality.

- **Document Changes:** Write meaningful commit messages for future reference.

Think of version control as having a detailed, step-by-step scrapbook of your baking adventures. You can revisit any step, see what you changed, and share your recipes with friends-confident that nothing gets lost and every improvement is preserved.

Version control is your code's safety net and creative playground. Whether you're solo or in a team, tools like Git and platforms like GitHub ensure you never lose your best work, always know what changed, and can collaborate without confusion. It's the secret ingredient for every successful software project!

8.2 Experiment Safely with Branching

Branching is your codebase's safety net-a way to try new ideas, fix bugs, or add features without disrupting the stable main branch. Think of your project like a tree: each branch is a separate line of development, letting you experiment freely while keeping the trunk (main branch) healthy and deployable.

How Branching Works

294

- **Create a Branch:** Start a new branch from the main branch for any new feature, bug fix, or experiment. For example:

  - `feature/add-chat-logic`

  - `fix/resolve-memory-leak`
    This isolates your work from the production-ready code.

- **Work in Isolation:** Make changes, test, and commit as much as needed on your branch. Your work won't affect others or the main branch until you're ready.

- **Short-Lived and Focused:** Keep branches small and short-lived-ideally just a couple of days-so merging back is easy and conflicts are minimized

- **Pull Requests and Code Review:** When your branch is ready, open a pull request. Teammates can review your changes, suggest improvements, and catch bugs before merging into the main branch

295

- **Merge and Clean Up:** Once approved, merge your changes into the main branch and delete the feature branch to keep things tidy

Branching Strategies

- **Feature Branches:** For new features or enhancements (`feature/add-logging`).

- **Bugfix Branches:** For fixing specific bugs (`bugfix/fix-login-error`).

- **Hotfix Branches:** For urgent fixes to production (`hotfix/patch-security-issue`)

Naming branches descriptively helps everyone know what's being worked on and why.

Why Use Branching?

- **Safe Experimentation:** Try out ideas without risking the stability of your main codebase.

- **Parallel Development:** Multiple team members can work on different features or fixes simultaneously

- **Simplified Code Reviews:** Isolated branches make it easier to review focused sets of changes

- **Easier Bug Tracking:** If a problem arises, it's clear which branch introduced it.

Best Practices

- **Keep Branches Short-Lived:** Merge back into main frequently to avoid complex conflicts and "merge hell"

- **One Task per Branch:** Focus each branch on a single feature or bug fix for clarity and easier review

297

- **Regularly Sync with Main:** Pull in the latest changes from main to your branch to minimize conflicts at merge time

- **Use Descriptive Names:** Make it clear what the branch is for (e.g., `feature/user-auth`, `fix/typo-in-readme`)

Branching lets you innovate and fix issues safely, keeping your main codebase stable. By using short-lived, focused branches and following a clear workflow, you make collaboration smoother, code reviews easier, and your project healthier overall.

8.3 Streamlined Collaboration

Platforms like GitHub have revolutionized how developers work together, acting as a shared workspace where multiple contributors can simultaneously develop, review, and refine code. With Git at the core, these platforms manage contributions efficiently, minimize conflicts, and provide clear visibility into who changed what and when.

298

Key Collaboration Features

1. Pull Requests (PRs):

Pull requests are central to collaborative workflows. They allow developers to propose changes, start discussions, and request code reviews before merging updates into the main branch. This process ensures that all contributions are vetted for quality and correctness, and that any potential issues are addressed early.

2. Branching:

Each contributor can work on their own branch, isolating features or bug fixes from the main codebase. This enables parallel development and reduces the risk of breaking the main project.

3. Code Review:

PRs facilitate code reviews, where teammates can comment on, suggest, or request changes to the code. This collaborative scrutiny helps maintain high standards and catch errors before they reach production.

4. Issues and Project Boards:

GitHub and similar platforms provide tools for tracking bugs, feature requests, and project progress. Issues can be linked to PRs, and project boards help teams organize and prioritize work.

5. Communication Tools:

Beyond code, platforms offer built-in discussion forums, comment threads, and notifications, keeping everyone informed and engaged.

How It Works in Practice

- **Invite Collaborators:** Add team members to your repository with specific permissions

- **Clone and Branch:** Each developer clones the repo and creates a branch for their work.

- **Develop and Commit:** Contributors make changes and commit them to their branch.

- **Open a Pull Request:** Changes are proposed via a PR, where teammates can review, discuss, and suggest improvements.

300

- **Merge After Review:** Once approved, the PR is merged into the main branch, keeping the codebase stable and up-to-date

Best Practices for Effective Collaboration

- Use descriptive branch names and commit messages.

- Keep PRs focused and small for easier review.

- Make code reviews a routine part of your workflow.

- Document processes and decisions in README files or wikis.

- Leverage automation (CI/CD) to test and validate changes before merging

Platforms like GitHub streamline teamwork by providing robust tools for version control, code review, project management, and communication. These features make it easy for teams to collaborate

301

efficiently, maintain code quality, and deliver better software together

8.4 Clear History with Commit Messages

Commits are snapshots of your project at specific points. Each commit should have a clear, concise message explaining what changed and why. Think of them as entries in a project diary or recipe instructions. Good commit messages (e.g., "feat: Add tokenizer for dataset X", "fix: Correct learning rate scheduler bug") make it easy for anyone (including your future self) to understand the project's evolution. Avoid vague notes; be descriptive but brief.

Teams at major AI labs like Hugging Face rely heavily on Git and GitHub to manage the development of countless models and libraries. They use branching extensively for experiments, rigorously review code via pull requests, and maintain clear commit histories to keep their massive, collaborative projects organized and progressing smoothly.

302

Best Practices for Version Control:

- **Commit Frequently:** Save your work often with meaningful commit messages. Small, focused commits are easier to understand and revert if needed.

- **Use a Structured Branching Strategy:** Adopt a consistent naming convention for branches (e.g., main, develop, feature/feature-name, bugfix/issue-number). Models like **Gitflow** can provide a robust structure, especially for larger teams or complex projects.

- **Prioritize Code Reviews:** Implement a mandatory code review process using pull requests before merging changes into main branches. This catches bugs, improves code quality, and facilitates knowledge sharing.

- **Maintain Consistent File Naming:** Use clear and consistent names for files and directories within your project (e.g., training_log_v1.md,

303

data_preprocessing_script.py) to improve organization.

By mastering version control, you establish a solid foundation for your project, enabling safe experimentation, smooth collaboration, and a clear, traceable history of your work.

8.5 Documentation: Your Project's Treasure Map

Documentation is like creating a detailed treasure map for your LLM project—it guides you, your team, and potentially others through the complexities, decisions, and outcomes of your work. Without it, revisiting your project months later can feel like digging blind, wondering why a specific hyperparameter was chosen or how a particular dataset was processed. Good documentation is the gateway to understanding the purpose, design, and evolution of your LLM training journey.

What to Document:

304

- **Project Goals & Scope:** Clearly state what the LLM is intended to do and its limitations.

- **Data Details:** Describe the data sources used, preprocessing steps taken (cleaning, tokenization, augmentation), dataset statistics, and any known biases.

- **Model Architecture:** Detail the model type (e.g., Transformer variant), number of layers, attention mechanisms, vocabulary size, and initialization methods.

- **Training Configuration:** Record hyperparameters (learning rate, batch size, optimizer), training duration, hardware used (GPUs/TPUs), and software frameworks/libraries with versions.

- **Experiments & Results:** Log experiments conducted, including variations in parameters or data. Record key metrics (loss, accuracy, perplexity) and evaluation results on validation/test sets. Tools like **Jupyter**

305

Notebooks are excellent for this, as they allow you to interleave code, explanations, and results in a structured logbook format.

- **Challenges & Solutions:** Document any problems encountered during training (e.g., overfitting, memory issues, slow convergence) and the steps taken to resolve them.

- **Deployment & Usage:** If applicable, provide instructions on how to use the trained model, including API details or setup requirements.

Keeping Documentation Tidy:

- **Organize Logically:** Structure your documentation intuitively. Use folders for different sections (e.g., /data, /models, /experiments, /docs). A clear hierarchy prevents information from getting lost.

- **Use Standard Formats:** Utilize formats like Markdown (.md) for easy readability and

306

compatibility with platforms like GitHub (README files).

- **Automate Where Possible:** Consider using documentation generator tools like **Sphinx** or **MkDocs**. These can automatically create professional-looking documentation websites from code comments (docstrings) and Markdown files, saving time and ensuring consistency.

- **Keep it Updated:** Documentation is only useful if it's current. Make it a habit to update documentation whenever significant changes are made to the code, data, or training process.

Many research papers from institutions like OpenAI or Google AI are accompanied by detailed appendices or supplementary materials (often shared via repositories) that document their experimental setup, datasets, and hyperparameters. This transparency allows others to understand, replicate, and build upon their work.

307

Best Practices for Documentation:

- **Document As You Go:** Don't leave documentation until the end. Jot down notes, comments in code, and experimental details while they are fresh in your mind.

- **Be Clear and Concise:** Write for your future self and potential collaborators. Avoid jargon where possible or define it clearly.

- **Include Visuals:** Use diagrams for model architecture or charts for results where appropriate.

- **Version Your Documentation:** Just like code, documentation should evolve. Track changes if necessary.

- **Use Notebooks for Experiment Logs:** Jupyter or similar notebooks are ideal for recording individual experiments, combining code execution, notes, and results in one place.

By maintaining detailed and organized documentation, you create an invaluable resource that ensures clarity, reproducibility, and easier maintenance for your LLM project, benefiting both yourself and anyone else involved.

8.6 Knowledge Sharing: Spreading the Love

Sharing what you learn during your LLM project is like passing around a fantastic recipe—it benefits the entire community, sparks new ideas, and prevents others from reinventing the wheel. In the fast-paced world of LLMs, fostering a culture of sharing accelerates innovation and collective progress.

Effective Ways to Share:

- **Code Repositories:** Platforms like **GitHub** or **GitLab** are the standard for sharing code. Create a well-documented public repository for your project, including a clear README.md file explaining what the project does, how to set it up, and how to use it. This allows others to easily

309

explore, use, and potentially contribute to your work.

- **Model Hubs:** Platforms like the **Hugging Face Hub** are specifically designed for sharing pre-trained models, datasets, and even live demos (**Spaces**). Uploading your model weights and configurations here makes them readily accessible to a vast audience.

- **Accessible Formats:** Share findings, tutorials, or analyses in easy-to-read formats like blog posts, **Jupyter Notebooks**, or **Markdown** files. Including code snippets and clear explanations makes complex concepts digestible. Think of it as providing both the finished cake and the recipe.

- **Tutorials & Blog Posts:** Writing a tutorial (e.g., "How I Fine-Tuned BERT for Sentiment Analysis") or a blog post detailing your process, challenges, and results provides valuable insights for others facing similar tasks.

310

The Hugging Face team exemplifies knowledge sharing. They host thousands of pre-trained models and datasets on their Hub, complete with model cards explaining their architecture and training. Their transformers library itself is open-source on GitHub. This collaborative ecosystem allows researchers and developers worldwide to stand on the shoulders of giants, fine-tuning models and sharing their improvements back with the community.

Best Practices for Sharing:

- **Document Thoroughly:** Accompany shared code or models with clear documentation (READMEs, model cards, comments) explaining usage, limitations, and methodology.

- **Use Clear Naming & Versioning:** Employ semantic versioning (e.g., v1.0.0, v1.1.0) using Git tags to mark releases and track the evolution of your shared assets. Consistent naming helps others understand the project's history.

311

- **Choose Appropriate Licenses:** Select an open-source license (e.g., MIT, Apache 2.0) for your shared code or models to clarify how others can use, modify, and distribute your work.

- **Keep Shared Resources Updated:** If you continue developing the project, update your shared repositories or model hubs periodically to reflect the latest improvements or fixes.

- **Example of Sharing a Small Project:** If you train a small model:

  - Push your code to a public GitHub repository (git push origin main).

  - Write a README.md explaining the model (e.g., "MyChatBot v1.0 - trained on 100 chats, LR 0.0001").

  - Tag the release (git tag v1.0 && git push origin v1.0).

  - (Bonus) Upload model weights to the Hugging Face Hub.

312

By actively sharing your knowledge, code, and models, you not only contribute to the broader LLM community but also gain visibility, receive feedback, and potentially foster new collaborations, ultimately accelerating innovation for everyone.

8.7 Communication and Collaboration: Teamwork Makes the Dream Work

While solo exploration is common in LLM development, many larger projects involve teams. In these cases, effective communication and collaboration are the glue holding everything together. It's like planning a group road trip: clear directions, shared supplies, and agreement on the route are essential for reaching the destination smoothly. Effective teamwork keeps LLM projects humming and prevents costly misunderstandings.

Maintaining Momentum:

- **Establish Clear Communication Channels:** Use dedicated tools like **Slack**, **Discord**, or **Microsoft Teams** for day-to-day discussions and quick

313

questions. Create specific channels (e.g., #llm-training-logs, #llm-data-pipeline) to keep conversations organized and focused.

- **Hold Regular Sync-Ups:** Schedule brief, regular meetings (e.g., daily stand-ups or weekly check-ins) to align the team on progress, roadblocks, and next steps. Share wins and challenges openly. Using a simple, shared agenda can keep these meetings focused and efficient.

- **Implement Code Reviews:** As mentioned under Version Control, code reviews via **pull requests** on platforms like GitHub are crucial for team projects. They ensure code quality, catch bugs early, enforce consistency, and serve as a valuable knowledge-sharing mechanism.

314

Effective Team Management Practices:

- **Foster Knowledge Sharing within the Team:** Encourage team members to share insights, helpful resources, code snippets, or solutions to problems encountered. Tools like a shared **Google Doc**, internal **Wiki** (e.g., Confluence), or dedicated Slack channel can facilitate this internal wisdom exchange.

- **Define Roles and Responsibilities (If Applicable):** Especially in larger teams, clarifying who is responsible for which aspect (data pipeline, model training, evaluation, deployment) can prevent overlap and ensure accountability.

- **Establish Conflict Resolution Processes:** Disagreements can happen. Having a predefined, respectful process for discussing differing opinions or technical approaches helps resolve conflicts constructively. Sometimes designating a neutral lead or facilitator can help.

315

- **Utilize Project Management Tools:** Tools like **Trello**, **Asana**, or **Jira** can help track tasks, assign ownership, set deadlines, and visualize project progress, keeping everyone informed and organized.

Large AI research labs and companies building foundational models rely heavily on structured communication and collaboration tools. Teams often use internal wikis for documentation, dedicated chat channels for specific sub-projects, rigorous code review processes, and project management software to coordinate the efforts of dozens or even hundreds of researchers and engineers, often working across different time zones.

Setting a Collaborative Rhythm:

Even for small teams, establishing routines helps:

- Use a primary chat tool (like Slack or Discord) for quick updates.

- Conduct short weekly meetings (e.g., via Zoom or Google Meet) to discuss progress and blockers.

316

- Make code reviews via pull requests a standard part of the workflow.

- Track major tasks and milestones using a shared tool (like Trello or a simple spreadsheet).

By prioritizing clear communication, structured collaboration, and effective project management, teams can navigate the complexities of LLM training much more efficiently, leading to higher quality results and a more positive development experience.

8.8 Building a Well-Oiled LLM Training Machine

And there you have it—your playbook for managing LLM training projects! Version control keeps your code safe and shareable, documentation maps out your journey, knowledge sharing spreads the love, and collaboration keeps the team humming. Together, these elements turn chaos into a smooth ride. By integrating these practices, you create a thriving ecosystem for AI research—one that streamlines your work and sets the stage for future breakthroughs.

317

You don't need to be a pro to start—just grab Git, jot some notes, share a snippet, and chat with your crew (or yourself!). Every step builds a stronger project—whether it's a tiny chatbot or the next GPT. So, fire up your laptop, organize your bits, and let's make some AI magic. You've got the tools—now go rock it!

318

CHAPTER 9: Overcoming Hardware Limitations: Making the Most of What You've Got

Training an LLM is a big job, and one of the toughest hurdles is hardware—especially GPU memory. It's like trying to fit a giant suitcase into a tiny car trunk: there's only so much room! When your model needs to juggle tons of data and calculations, memory can overflow fast. Let's explore a clever trick to dodge this problem: gradient checkpointing. One of the most significant hurdles in LLM training is the limited GPU memory available. Training large models requires storing extensive amounts of data for computations, which often leads to memory overflow issues. It's like trying to fit an elephant into a Mini Cooper: you need to find creative ways to make it work.

9.1 Gradient Checkpointing: Recomputing for Savings

Gradient checkpointing is a powerful technique for training large neural networks on limited hardware, especially when GPU memory is the main bottleneck.

319

Think of it like solving a massive jigsaw puzzle on a small table: instead of spreading out all the pieces (activations), you keep just a few key pieces visible and recompute the rest as needed. This approach trades extra computation for significant memory savings, enabling you to train bigger models on smaller GPUs

How Gradient Checkpointing Works

In standard neural network training, every intermediate activation (the outputs of each layer during the forward pass) is stored in memory so gradients can be computed during the backward pass. This approach quickly fills up GPU memory, especially for deep or complex models. Gradient checkpointing addresses this issue by saving only a subset of these activations, known as "checkpoints." When the backward pass requires an activation that wasn't stored, it is recomputed on-the-fly from the nearest checkpoint, rather than retrieved from memory. As a result, this method significantly reduces memory usage, allowing for the training of larger models or the use of bigger batch sizes that would otherwise be infeasible due to

320

memory constraints. However, there is a trade-off: some operations are performed more than once, leading to increased computation time-typically slowing training by 15–25%. Gradient checkpointing is widely supported in deep learning frameworks like PyTorch and is a powerful tool for optimizing memory

Memory vs. Computation Trade-off

Gradient checkpointing introduces a trade-off between memory usage and computation. By saving only a subset of activations and recomputing others as needed during backpropagation, you can typically reduce memory usage by 50–80%, depending on the model architecture and checkpointing strategy. However, this memory efficiency comes at the cost of increased computation: training may slow down by 20–40% because some operations are performed more than once during the backward pass. In practice, this trade-off is often worthwhile if memory is your primary constraint, as it enables you to use larger batch sizes or train deeper models than would otherwise fit on your hardware. For many deep learning practitioners, the

321

ability to train larger or more complex models outweighs the moderate increase in computation time.

Implementation Example (PyTorch & Hugging Face)

PyTorch:

```python
import torch
from torch.utils.checkpoint import checkpoint

def custom_forward(*inputs):
    # Define the forward pass for a part of your model
    return model_part(*inputs)

output = checkpoint(custom_forward, input_tensor)
```

output = checkpoint(custom_forward, input_tensor)

You wrap parts of your model with checkpoint, and PyTorch handles the recomputation automatically.

322

Hugging Face Transformers:

```python
from transformers import TrainingArguments, Trainer

training_args = TrainingArguments(
    per_device_train_batch_size=1,
    gradient_accumulation_steps=4,
    gradient_checkpointing=True,  # Just enable the flag!
    # ... other args
)
trainer = Trainer(model=model, args=training_args, train_dataset=dataset)
trainer.train()
```

Just set `gradient_checkpointing=True` in your training arguments, and the library does the rest.

Best Practices & Tips

- **Test with Small Batches:** Start with a small batch size to find the right balance between memory savings and computation time

- **Strategic Checkpoint Placement:** Uniform checkpointing (every few layers) is simple; adaptive strategies (based on layer complexity) can optimize memory even further

323

- **Monitor Training Speed:** Expect some slowdown; combine with other optimizations (like mixed precision) if needed

- **Framework Support:** PyTorch, TensorFlow, and Hugging Face all support gradient checkpointing, often with just a simple flag or wrapper function.

Summary Table

Approach	Memory Usage	Computation Time	Use Case
Standard Backpropagation	High	Normal	Small/medium models
Gradient Checkpointing	Low	Higher	Large models, limited hardware

Gradient checkpointing is a practical way to "tame" memory usage for deep learning, letting you train larger models or use bigger batch sizes on modest GPUs-just be ready for a bit more computation time as the trade-off.

9.2 Reducing Memory Usage: Squeezing More from Your Resources

Even with gradient checkpointing, some large language models (LLMs) can easily exceed the memory limits of a single GPU. To fit these "memory-hungry" models into

324

limited hardware-much like packing a tiny suitcase for a big trip-you need to use a combination of creative and technical strategies. Here are proven techniques to further reduce memory usage without sacrificing model performance.

1. Lower Precision (Quantization)

Lower precision, or quantization, is a technique that reduces the numerical precision of model weights and activations from the standard 32-bit floating point (float32) to lower bit-widths such as 16-bit (float16), 8-bit, or even 4-bit integers. This reduction means that each parameter in the model consumes less memory, often leading to memory savings of 50–75% with minimal or no loss in accuracy. Quantization enables the deployment and execution of large language models on hardware that might otherwise be unable to accommodate them. Popular methods like GPTQ, QLoRA, and Adaptive-Quant can quantize LLM weights to 4 or 8 bits, making it feasible to run models that would otherwise be too large for your available resources. These approaches are widely used in practice and have demonstrated strong performance, with some methods even matching or exceeding the accuracy of full-precision fine-tuning in certain tasks.

2. Flash Attention and Efficient Attention Mechanisms

Flash Attention and other efficient attention mechanisms are designed to address the memory and computational bottlenecks of self-attention layers in large language models (LLMs). Flash Attention is a memory-efficient algorithm that processes attention in smaller blocks, optimizing memory access patterns and reducing the need for repeated data transfers between high-bandwidth GPU memory and faster on-chip memory. While standard attention mechanisms scale quadratically with sequence length-quickly exhausting memory for long inputs-Flash Attention achieves linear scaling by dividing computations into manageable chunks and fusing operations, allowing models to handle much longer prompts without running out of memory. This approach not only lowers memory usage but also increases training and inference speed, with

326

no loss in output quality compared to standard attention.

Beyond Flash Attention, other innovations further improve efficiency. Sparse attention mechanisms compute attention over only a subset of tokens, making it possible to process extremely long texts with less memory and computation. Multi-query attention (MQA) reduces memory needs by sharing key-value pairs across multiple queries, significantly cutting down the number of key-value pairs that must be stored and accessed during inference. Together, these advancements enable LLMs to scale to longer sequences and larger models, making them more practical and efficient on modern hardware.

3. Model Architecture Innovations

Model architecture innovations have played a crucial role in reducing memory requirements and improving the efficiency of large language models. One major advancement is parameter sharing, as implemented in models like ALBERT, which reuse weights across layers

327

rather than assigning unique parameters to each layer. This approach can dramatically reduce the total number of parameters—by up to 89% compared to models like BERT—while maintaining or even improving performance on several NLP benchmarks. By sharing parameters, ALBERT achieves a much smaller memory footprint and faster training times, making it feasible to scale models without overwhelming hardware resources.

Another innovation is the use of sparse and windowed attention mechanisms. Instead of having every token attend to every other token, which is computationally and memory intensive, these methods restrict attention to local windows or a sparse subset of tokens. This significantly lowers both compute and memory requirements, enabling models to handle longer sequences and larger contexts more efficiently.

Multi-Query Attention (MQA) is yet another memory-saving technique, where key-value projections are shared across multiple attention heads. This approach slashes the memory needed for key-value caches,

328

reducing storage from gigabytes to just megabytes when working with long contexts. Together, these architectural strategies allow for the development and deployment of much larger and more capable language models, even on hardware with limited memory resources.

4. Pruning

Pruning is a technique used to reduce the size and complexity of neural networks by removing redundant or less important weights from the model. By eliminating these unnecessary parameters-often determined through magnitude-based methods that target weights with the smallest absolute values-pruned models become smaller and faster, consuming less memory while typically maintaining much of their original accuracy. This makes them especially useful for deployment on resource-constrained devices or in real-time applications. Magnitude-based pruning is one of the most widely used approaches and is supported by popular frameworks such as TensorFlow Lite, allowing developers to efficiently compress models for practical use without significant performance loss.

5. Parallelization

Parallelization techniques are essential for handling large models that exceed the memory capacity of a single GPU. Model parallelism involves splitting the model across multiple GPUs so that each device is responsible for storing and processing only a portion of the network. This approach enables the training or inference of models that would otherwise be too large to fit on a single GPU. In addition, tensor parallelism takes this concept further by dividing large tensors, such as weight matrices, across multiple devices. This further distributes the memory load and allows for even larger models to be trained efficiently. Together, model and tensor parallelism maximize hardware utilization and make it feasible to work with state-of-the-art language models on available GPU clusters.

6. Efficient KV Cache Management

330

Efficient key-value (KV) cache management is crucial for optimizing memory usage during inference in large language models. In transformer architectures, the KV cache stores intermediate states-specifically, the key and value vectors generated during each step of autoregressive text generation-so that these do not have to be recomputed for every new token. This dramatically reduces redundant computation and speeds up inference, but the memory required for the KV cache grows linearly with the sequence length, the number of layers, and the number of attention heads, quickly becoming a bottleneck for long-context or high-throughput applications. To address this, modern systems implement strategies such as storing only the necessary KV entries, employing sliding windows or cache eviction policies to discard the oldest or least useful states, and supporting multi-sequence caching for shared prefixes.

Innovations like Multi-Query Attention (MQA) further reduce KV cache memory needs by sharing key-value projections across attention heads, shrinking the cache

331

size from gigabytes to megabytes for long contexts and enabling larger batch sizes. Advanced frameworks, such as InfiniGen, dynamically manage and prefetch only essential cache entries, significantly improving performance and memory efficiency for long-text generation. Overall, efficient KV cache management allows LLMs to generate longer sequences and serve more users simultaneously, making large-scale inference feasible even on memory-constrained hardware.

7. Universal Transformer Memory & Adaptive Quantization

Universal Transformer Memory and adaptive quantization are two advanced techniques for improving memory efficiency in large language models. Universal Transformer Memory, as implemented in approaches like Neural Attention Memory Models (NAMMs), uses neural networks to selectively retain only the most relevant information in the model's memory, discarding unnecessary bits. This learned memory management system enables transformers to focus on the most important contexts for each layer and attention head, which can slash memory costs by up to 75% without sacrificing performance. NAMMs have demonstrated strong results across long-context benchmarks, and their benefits generalize to various transformer architectures and even other modalities such as vision and reinforcement learning.

Adaptive quantization, on the other hand, dynamically adjusts the level of quantization for different parts of the model, optimizing the trade-off between memory usage and accuracy. Recent advances like AQUA-KV exploit dependencies between key and value vectors in transformer caches, allowing for highly compressed representations-sometimes as low as 2–2.5 bits per value-while preserving near-lossless accuracy even on large models such as Llama 3. By combining selective memory retention with adaptive quantization, these innovations make it possible to deploy and run state-of-the-art language models far more efficiently, especially in memory-constrained environments.

333

Summary Table: Key Memory-Saving Techniques

Technique	Memory Savings	Impact on Performance	Typical Use Case
Lower Precision (Quantization)	50-75%	Minimal accuracy loss	Training & inference
Flash/Sparse Attention	Up to 80%+	No/little loss	Long sequence processing
Parameter Sharing	Up to 90%	Some accuracy tradeoff	Lightweight models (e.g. ALBERT)
Pruning	10-50%	Minimal if done well	Edge deployment, inference
Model/Tensor Parallelism	Unlimited (scales)	None if well balanced	Multi-GPU setups
Efficient KV Caching	10-90%	None to minimal	Inference, long contexts
Universal Transformer Memory	Up to 75%	Minimal	Cutting-edge LLM optimization

By combining these methods-quantization, Flash Attention, architectural tweaks, pruning, parallelism, and smart cache management-you can dramatically squeeze more out of your hardware, enabling even the largest LLMs to run efficiently on modest resources.

9.3 Using bfloat16: The Lightweight Numbers

Training large models with 32-bit floating point numbers (float32) is like carrying heavy, hardcover books-precise but bulky and resource-intensive. **bfloat16** offers a smarter, lighter alternative: it uses just 16 bits per number, cutting memory usage in half

334

while keeping nearly all the dynamic range and practical accuracy needed for deep learning

What Is bfloat16?

- **bfloat16** (brain floating point 16) is a 16-bit floating point format designed for machine learning.

- It uses 1 bit for the sign, 8 bits for the exponent (same as float32), and 7 bits for the mantissa (less precise than float32, which has 23 bits)

- This structure gives bfloat16 the **same range** as float32 (about $\pm 3.4 \times 1038 \pm 3.4 \times 1038$), but with less decimal precision

Why Use bfloat16?

- **Cuts Memory Usage in Half:** Each parameter, activation, and gradient takes up 16 bits instead of 32, so you can fit much larger models or batch sizes on the same hardware

335

- **Maintains Dynamic Range:** Unlike float16, bfloat16's exponent size matches float32, so it avoids overflow/underflow issues and can represent very large or small numbers safely

- **Minimal Accuracy Loss:** For most deep learning tasks, the reduced precision of bfloat16 has little or no effect on model accuracy, especially when used in mixed precision training where critical operations still use float32.

- **Faster Training:** Many modern GPUs and TPUs are optimized for bfloat16, offering significant speedups during training

- **Numerical Stability:** bfloat16 is less prone to producing NaN or Inf errors than float16, making training more robust for large models.

336

Practical Usage

How bfloat16 Compares to Other Formats

Format	Bits	Exponent Bits	Mantissa Bits	Dynamic Range	Precision	Memory Use
float32	32	8	23	$\pm 3.4 \times 10^{38}$	High	High
float16	16	5	10	$\pm 6.55 \times 10^{4}$	Moderate	Low
bfloat16	16	8	7	$\pm 3.4 \times 10^{38}$	Lower (but enough)	Low

- **Mixed Precision Training:** Most frameworks (PyTorch, TensorFlow) use bfloat16 for forward/backward passes and float32 for weight updates, balancing speed, memory, and accuracy

- **Hardware Support:** bfloat16 is widely supported on modern GPUs (NVIDIA A100, H100) and TPUs, making it a practical choice for LLMs and other large models.

9.4 Model Compression: Slimming Down

Model compression is like trimming a bush: you cut away the excess while preserving the essential shape and function. For large language models (LLMs), compression techniques help make models more efficient-reducing memory usage, speeding up

337

inference, and enabling deployment on resource-constrained devices-without significant loss in accuracy.

Key Model Compression Techniques

1. Pruning

Pruning is a technique that removes unnecessary or less important weights from a neural network, often by setting them to zero. This process can be guided by various criteria, such as the magnitude of the weights, activation patterns, or other importance measures. The primary benefit of pruning is that it produces a sparse model, which uses less memory and can run faster, particularly when hardware or software supports efficient sparse matrix operations. For example, NeuralWave Solutions successfully pruned their large language model (LLM) to run efficiently on edge devices like smart speakers, maintaining high performance while significantly reducing the model's memory footprint.

2. Quantization

338

Quantization is a technique that reduces the numerical precision of model weights and activations, typically converting them from 32-bit floating point representations to 8-bit or even lower. By storing weights with fewer bits, quantization not only decreases the overall model size but also speeds up computations, making both training and inference more efficient. The benefits include halving or even quartering memory usage and accelerating inference times, usually with minimal impact on model accuracy. Quantization can be applied after training (post-training quantization) or incorporated during training through quantization-aware training. For example, Tech Research Labs adopted the bfloat16 (a 16-bit format) for their large language model, enabling it to fit on a single GPU and significantly boosting processing speed without the need for expensive hardware upgrades.

3. Low-Rank Factorization

Low-rank factorization is a model compression technique that approximates large weight matrices in neural networks by expressing them as products of

339

smaller matrices, also known as low-rank approximations. Techniques such as Singular Value Decomposition (SVD) are commonly used to decompose a weight matrix into components with lower rank, significantly reducing the number of parameters and computational requirements. This approach is especially effective for compressing dense layers, where the majority of a model's parameters are often concentrated, and it can also accelerate matrix multiplications during inference and training. By exploiting redundancies within the weight matrices, low-rank factorization maintains model performance while reducing memory usage-studies have shown parameter reductions of 30–50% or more with minimal accuracy loss. This technique is widely used for making large language models and deep neural networks more efficient and deployable on resource-constrained hardware.

4. Knowledge Distillation

Knowledge distillation is a model compression technique that trains a smaller "student" model to

340

mimic the outputs of a larger, more complex "teacher" model. The student model learns to reproduce the teacher's behavior—often by matching the probability distributions (soft labels) generated by the teacher— thereby capturing much of the teacher's performance in a more compact form. This process results in lightweight models that are ideal for deployment on mobile or edge devices, where memory and computational resources are limited.

For example, Tech Research Labs used bfloat16 precision to halve memory usage, enabling a large language model to fit on a single GPU and speeding up experimentation. AI Startups Inc. employed gradient clipping and model compression to train a large language model on a mid-range GPU, achieving stable and crash-free training. NeuralWave Solutions combined pruning and quantization to deploy their language model on smart speakers, maintaining high performance while significantly reducing the model size. Overall, knowledge distillation enables the creation of efficient, deployable models that retain

341

much of the accuracy and capability of their larger counterparts, making advanced AI more accessible and practical for real-world applications.

Pruning vs. Quantization: Which to Choose?

- *Quantization* generally provides higher compression ratios with less impact on accuracy, especially for moderate compression

- *Pruning* is more effective at very high compression rates or when model sparsity is critical, but may require more fine-tuning to maintain performance

- Both techniques can be combined or used alongside other methods like low-rank factorization and knowledge distillation for even greater efficiency.

342

Summary Table: Common Model Compression Techniques

Technique	How It Works	Memory Savings	Impact on Accuracy	Best Use Case
Pruning	Remove unimportant weights	Moderate–High	Minimal–Moderate	Edge devices, sparse computation
Quantization	Lower weights/activation precision	High	Minimal	General deployment, fast inference
Low-Rank Factorization	Matrix decomposition	Moderate	Minimal–Moderate	Large dense layers
Knowledge Distillation	Train smaller student model	High	Minimal	Mobile, embedded, edge devices

Model compression is a practical, flexible toolkit for making LLMs leaner and more deployable. By pruning, quantizing, and distilling, you can dramatically reduce memory and compute needs-making AI smarter, faster, and more accessible.

9.5 Scaling Up with Distributed Training: The Power of Teamwork

Training a large language model (LLM) is a monumental task-like running a marathon by yourself. It's time-consuming, exhausting for your hardware, and sometimes simply impossible with a single device. **Distributed training** changes the game by bringing in a team: you split the workload across multiple GPUs or

343

TPUs, turning that solo marathon into a high-speed relay race.

What Is Distributed Training?

Distributed training is the process of dividing a machine learning workload across several computing devices (GPUs, TPUs, or even entire servers). This allows you to:

- **Train larger models** that wouldn't fit on a single device.

- **Process bigger batches** and datasets for faster convergence.

- **Reduce training time** from weeks or months to days or even hours.

How Distributed Training Works

1. Data Parallelism

- **Each device gets a copy of the model** and processes a unique chunk of the data.

344

- **Gradients are averaged** (synchronized) after each batch, so all devices update their models in unison.

- **Best for:** When your model fits on a single device, but your dataset is huge.

2. Model Parallelism

- **The model itself is split** across multiple devices, with each device responsible for a different part (e.g., different layers).

- **Data flows through devices sequentially,** allowing you to train models too large for any single GPU.

- **Best for:** Extremely large models that exceed single-device memory.

3. Hybrid Parallelism

- **Combines data and model parallelism** for maximum flexibility and efficiency.

345

- **Used in:** Cutting-edge LLM training (e.g., GPT-4, PaLM).

Benefits of Distributed Training

- **Speed:** Dramatically reduces wall-clock training time.

- **Scale:** Enables training of models and datasets that would be impossible on a single device.

- **Efficiency:** Makes full use of available hardware, reducing idle time and energy waste.

- **Collaboration:** Multiple researchers or teams can work together, sharing resources and expertise.

Think of distributed training like a relay race:

- Each runner (GPU/TPU) covers part of the distance.

- The baton (model/data) is passed efficiently between teammates.

346

- The team finishes the race much faster than any one runner could alone.

Popular Distributed Training Frameworks

- **PyTorch Distributed Data Parallel (DDP):** Easy, robust, and widely used for both data and model parallelism.

- **TensorFlow MirroredStrategy and MultiWorkerMirroredStrategy:** For seamless scaling in TensorFlow.

- **Horovod:** Framework-agnostic, supports TensorFlow, PyTorch, and MXNet.

- **DeepSpeed and Megatron-LM:** Specialized for massive LLMs, providing advanced optimizations for memory and compute.

Best Practices for Distributed Training

When it comes to distributed training, there are several best practices to ensure efficiency and stability. It's recommended to start with data parallelism, as it is the

347

easiest to implement and can deliver significant speedups in training. However, it's important to monitor communication overhead, since excessive data transfer between devices can become a bottleneck; this can be mitigated by optimizing batch sizes and ensuring sufficient network bandwidth. Regular synchronization of devices is crucial to prevent model divergence and maintain consistent training progress across all nodes. Additionally, using mixed precision training-combining data types such as bfloat16 or float16 with standard precision-not only saves memory but also accelerates training, making it a valuable technique for large-scale distributed setups.

Summary Table: Distributed Training Approaches

Approach	Model Size	Data Size	Speedup Potential	Complexity	Use Case
Data Parallel	Small–Large	Large	High	Low	Most LLM training
Model Parallel	Huge	Any	Moderate	Medium–High	Very large models (GPT-4, etc.)
Hybrid Parallel	Huge	Huge	Highest	High	State-of-the-art LLMs

Distributed training is the ultimate teamwork strategy for machine learning. By splitting the workload across multiple devices, you can train larger models, process more data, and finish faster than ever before-turning what once seemed impossible into a routine achievement.

9.6 Data Parallelism: Dividing the Data Load

Data parallelism is the most widely used approach for distributed training in deep learning. Imagine splitting a big homework assignment among several friends-each person tackles a different section, and then you combine the results. In data parallelism, **each GPU (or compute node) holds a full copy of the model**, but processes a different chunk (mini-batch) of the training data at the same time. After processing, the GPUs synchronize their updates (gradients) before collectively updating the model parameters. This parallelism dramatically speeds up training by processing more data simultaneously.

How Data Parallelism Works

1. **Model Replication:**
   Each GPU gets an identical copy of the model.

349

- **Data Splitting:**
  The training dataset is divided into smaller chunks (mini-batches), with each GPU receiving a different chunk to process in parallel.

- **Independent Computation:**
  Each GPU computes the forward and backward pass on its data, calculating gradients independently.

- **Gradient Synchronization:**
  After each mini-batch, gradients from all GPUs are averaged (using an "all-reduce" operation) so every model copy stays in sync.

- This ensures that, after each update, all GPUs have identical model weights.

- **Parameter Update:**
  Synchronized gradients are used to update the model parameters collectively, maintaining consistency across all devices

5. . **Benefits of Data Parallelism**

350

- **Faster Training:** Multiple GPUs process data in parallel, reducing overall training time

- **Scalability:** Easily scales from two GPUs to dozens or more, as resources allow

- **Simplicity:** Well-supported by modern frameworks (like PyTorch's DistributedDataParallel), making setup and management straightforward

351

Implementation Example: PyTorch
DistributedDataParallel (DDP)

```python
import torch
import torch.distributed as dist
from torch.nn.parallel import DistributedDataParallel as DDP

def main():
    dist.init_process_group("nccl")  # Initialize communication
    rank = dist.get_rank()
    torch.cuda.set_device(rank)
    model = MyModel().to(rank)
    ddp_model = DDP(model, device_ids=[rank])
    optimizer = torch.optim.Adam(ddp_model.parameters())

    for data, target in train_loader:
        data, target = data.to(rank), target.to(rank)
        optimizer.zero_grad()
        output = ddp_model(data)
        loss = loss_fn(output, target)
        loss.backward()
        optimizer.step()

    dist.destroy_process_group()
```

Best Practices

- **Batch Size:** Total batch size should be large enough to be split across all GPUs efficiently

- **Communication:** Minimize communication overhead by using efficient libraries like NCCL for gradient synchronization

- **Fault Tolerance:** Monitor for failed nodes and use checkpointing to avoid losing progress.

- **Framework Support:** Use built-in tools like PyTorch's DDP or TensorFlow's MirroredStrategy for robust, scalable training.

Data parallelism is like teamwork for your GPUs-each device tackles a slice of the data, and by synchronizing

Summary Table: Data Parallelism Workflow

Step	What Happens
Model Replication	Each GPU gets a full model copy
Data Splitting	Dataset is divided across GPUs
Independent Training	Each GPU computes forward/backward pass
Gradient Sync	Gradients are averaged (all-reduce)
Parameter Update	All models update weights identically

353

their progress, you achieve faster, more efficient training. Frameworks like PyTorch make it easy to implement, so you can start small and scale up as your resources grow.

9.7 Model Parallelism: Splitting the Model

When your model is so massive that it can't fit into the memory of a single GPU-even after applying memory-saving tricks like gradient checkpointing-**model parallelism** becomes essential. Think of it as assembling a giant, complex puzzle: instead of one person struggling to manage all the pieces, you divide the puzzle into sections, with different people (GPUs) working on each part. In model parallelism, different layers or blocks of the neural network are distributed across multiple GPUs, and data flows sequentially through these parts during both the forward and backward passes.

How Model Parallelism Works

- **Partitioning the Model:** The neural network is divided so that each GPU is responsible for

354

specific layers or components. For example, the first few layers might be on GPU 0, the next set on GPU 1, and so on

- **Sequential Data Flow:** During training, input data passes through the model sections on each GPU in sequence. Intermediate outputs (activations) are transferred between devices as needed

- **Forward and Backward Passes:** Both the forward and backward computations require communication between GPUs, since each only has part of the model

Types of Model Parallelism

- **Pipeline Parallelism:** The model is split into "stages," each assigned to a different GPU. Micro-batches of data are pipelined through these stages, like an assembly line, to maximize hardware utilization and throughput

355

- **Tensor Parallelism:** Large tensors (such as weight matrices) are split horizontally across GPUs, with each device processing a shard in parallel. This is especially useful for very wide layers

Benefit	Description
Enables Training of Huge Models	Allows you to train models that exceed the memory of any single GPU
Flexibility in Architecture	Supports complex, custom model designs
Reduces Bottlenecks	Distributes computation, reducing memory and compute bottlenecks

Challenge	Description
Communication Overhead	Frequent data transfer between GPUs can slow down training
Implementation Complexity	Requires careful partitioning and management of data flow
Sequential Dependencies	GPUs may have to wait for each other, reducing parallel efficiency

Practical Implementation

- **Frameworks:** Libraries like DeepSpeed, Hugging Face Transformers, and Amazon SageMaker offer built-in support for model parallelism and pipeline parallelism, helping to manage the complexity of splitting models and coordinating data flow

356

- **Testing:** Always start with a small cluster or a simplified version of your model to validate your setup. Ensure data dependencies and inter-device communication are handled smoothly before scaling up to a larger cluster

Quantum AI Solutions used distributed training across a GPU cluster for their large-scale LLM. By combining data parallelism (splitting the data) and model parallelism (splitting the model), they reduced training time from months to weeks compared to using a single high-end machine.

Model vs. Data Parallelism: Quick Comparison

Feature	Data Parallelism	Model Parallelism
What's Split?	Data (mini-batches)	Model (layers/blocks/tensors)
Model Copy per GPU?	Yes (full model on each GPU)	No (each GPU has only a part of the model)
Communication	Gradients synchronized after each step	Activations/outputs passed between GPUs
Best For	Large datasets, moderate model sizes	Extremely large models
Complexity	Lower	Higher

Hybrid Approaches

For the largest LLMs, teams often combine data parallelism, model parallelism, and even tensor parallelism to maximize efficiency and scalability, overcoming both memory and compute bottlenecks

Model parallelism is the key to training truly gigantic models that would otherwise be impossible to fit on a single GPU. By strategically splitting the model across multiple devices-and using tools to manage the complexity-you can unlock new scales of AI performance and efficiency

9.8 Beyond the Basics: Tackling Other Tricky Bits

Training large language models (LLMs) isn't just about hardware and scaling-two persistent challenges that can derail even the most robust training runs are **overfitting** and **bias**. Addressing these issues is crucial for building models that are both accurate and fair.

Overfitting: When Your Model Memorizes Instead of Generalizes

What is Overfitting?

Overfitting happens when an LLM performs exceptionally well on its training data but fails to generalize to new, unseen examples. Signs include:

- High accuracy on training data, but poor results on validation or test sets.

- Inconsistent or repetitive responses to unfamiliar prompts.

- Poor real-world performance despite strong training metrics

Why Does Overfitting Happen?

- Small or unbalanced datasets.

- Excessive fine-tuning or too many training iterations.

359

- Overly complex models that latch onto noise or irrelevant patterns

How to Prevent Overfitting:

- **Curate Diverse, Balanced Data:** Use datasets with varied styles, topics, and contexts to encourage broader learning and reduce reliance on narrow patterns

- **Early Stopping:** Monitor validation performance and halt training before the model starts memorizing noise

- **Regularization:** Apply techniques like dropout (randomly disabling neurons during training) and weight decay (penalizing large weights) to limit model complexity

- **Cross-Validation:** Test the model on multiple data splits to ensure consistent performance across different subsets

- **Data Augmentation:** Slightly modify training data (e.g., paraphrasing, shuffling) to expose the model to more variety

- **Limit Fine-Tuning Iterations:** Avoid excessive updating, which can cause the model to lose its generalization ability

- **Monitor with Multiple Metrics:** Use a suite of evaluation metrics (accuracy, F1, perplexity) to get a holistic view of model performance

Bias: Ensuring Fairness and Reducing Harm

What is Bias in LLMs?

Bias occurs when a model's outputs reflect or amplify stereotypes, prejudices, or imbalances present in the training data. This can manifest as racial, gender, religious, or professional stereotypes, and can harm users or reinforce unfair societal patterns.

Why Does Bias Occur?

- LLMs are trained on large, often unfiltered datasets from the internet, which contain both subtle and overt biases

- Imbalanced data or lack of diversity in training samples can skew model outputs

How to Mitigate Bias:

- **Bias Detection and Evaluation:** Use dedicated benchmarks, metrics, and datasets to measure bias at various levels (embeddings, probabilities, generated text)

- **Data Curation:** Proactively filter, balance, and augment datasets to reduce the presence of harmful stereotypes

- **Bias Mitigation Techniques:**

- **Pre-processing:** Remove or rebalance biased examples before training.

- **In-training:** Apply regularization, adversarial training, or custom loss functions (e.g., Direct

362

Preference Optimization) to penalize biased outputs

- **Post-processing:** Adjust generated outputs or apply filters to correct bias after model inference

- **Feedback Loops:** Continuously monitor outputs, collect user feedback, and retrain or fine-tune the model to address new or emerging biases

- **Model Auditing:** Regularly audit model outputs for fairness and document known limitations

Emerging Solutions:

Recent research shows promise in using bias classifiers (e.g., BERT-based models) to detect and score bias in LLM outputs, then fine-tune the LLM using this feedback to reduce bias while monitoring for any trade-offs in performance.

Summary Table: Tackling Overfitting and Bias

Challenge	Why It Matters	Solutions & Best Practices
Overfitting	Poor generalization, unreliable	Diverse data, early stopping, regularization, cross-validation, data augmentation, limit fine-tuning
Bias	Unfair, harmful outputs	Data curation, bias evaluation, in-training and post-training mitigation, feedback loops, model auditing

No LLM training journey is free from bumps. By proactively addressing overfitting and bias-with robust data practices, regular evaluation, and targeted mitigation-you can build models that are not only powerful, but also reliable and fair in real-world applications.

9.9 Overfitting: When the Model Memorizes, Not Learns

One common pitfall is overfitting. This happens when your model becomes too specialized in the training data, essentially memorizing it rather than learning the underlying general patterns. Think of a student who crams for a specific test by memorizing every single practice question and answer; they might ace that test but fail miserably when faced with slightly different questions on the same topic because they didn't grasp the concepts. An overfit LLM performs exceptionally

364

well on the data it was trained on but fails to generalize to new, unseen text.

To combat overfitting, **regularization techniques** are essential. **Dropout** is a popular method where, during training, some neurons in the network are randomly "dropped out" or ignored for each training example. This forces the network to learn more robust representations that don't rely too heavily on any single neuron. Another effective technique is **early stopping**. Monitor the model's performance on a separate validation dataset (data it hasn't been trained on) throughout the training process. When the performance on the validation set stops improving or starts to worsen, even if the training loss is still decreasing, stop the training. This prevents the model from continuing to specialize only on the training data. Adding dropout layers within your model architecture (easily done in frameworks like PyTorch or TensorFlow) and implementing early stopping based on validation metrics are practical ways to keep overfitting in check.

Combating Overfitting: Essential Techniques

1. Regularization

- **Dropout:** Randomly disables a subset of neurons during each training step, forcing the model to learn more robust, distributed representations

- **Weight Decay (L2 Regularization):** Adds a penalty to the loss function based on the magnitude of the weights, discouraging overly complex models with large weights

2. Early Stopping

- Monitor the model's performance on a separate validation set during training.

- Stop training when validation performance plateaus or worsens, even if training loss continues to decrease. This prevents the model from continuing to specialize only on the training data

3. Data Augmentation

- Expand the training data by creating modified versions of the existing data (e.g., paraphrasing, back translation, shuffling)

- This exposes the model to more variety, making it harder to simply memorize and easier to generalize.

4. Increase Training Data and Diversity

- Use larger, more diverse datasets to reduce the chance of memorization and encourage learning of general patterns

- Balance datasets to include a wide range of writing styles, topics, and contexts.

5. Reduce Model Complexity

- Simplify the model architecture or reduce the number of parameters if possible, especially when working with smaller datasets

6. Cross-Validation

- Evaluate the model on multiple data splits to ensure it performs well across different subsets, not just the training data

Practical Steps for LLM Practitioners

- **Add Dropout Layers:** Most deep learning frameworks (like PyTorch or TensorFlow) make it easy to add dropout to your model architecture.

- **Implement Early Stopping:** Use callbacks or monitoring tools to halt training when validation metrics stop improving.

- **Regularly Validate:** Always check model performance on held-out data, not just training loss.

- **Curate and Augment Data:** Continuously update and diversify your dataset to keep the model learning broadly applicable patterns.

368

Summary Table: Overfitting Solutions

Technique	How It Helps
Dropout	Prevents reliance on specific neurons
Weight Decay	Discourages overly complex models
Early Stopping	Stops training before memorization occurs
Data Augmentation	Increases data variety; promotes generalization
Increase Data Size	Reduces risk of memorization
Reduce Complexity	Limits model's capacity to memorize
Cross-Validation	Ensures robustness across data splits

Overfitting is like cramming for a test-great for memorizing, bad for real-world performance. By applying regularization, early stopping, data augmentation, and careful monitoring, you can ensure your LLM truly learns, not just memorizes, and is ready to tackle new, unseen challenges.

9.10 Bias: Reflecting Flaws in the Data

Large Language Models learn from the data they are fed, and unfortunately, large datasets often contain societal biases present in the real world. An LLM trained primarily on technical documentation might struggle with nuances of poetry, while one trained on historical texts might inadvertently learn and perpetuate outdated or harmful stereotypes. Imagine

369

training an AI assistant only on conversations from one specific demographic group; it would likely struggle to interact naturally or fairly with people outside that group. Ensuring the model is fair and performs equitably across different contexts is crucial.

Addressing bias often starts with the data. While creating a perfectly unbiased dataset is extremely difficult, strive for diversity in your data sources. Incorporating text from various domains, styles, authors, and demographics can help. Techniques like **data augmentation** can sometimes be used to create more balanced synthetic data, though care must be taken not to introduce new biases. Utilizing **public datasets like Wikipedia or Common Crawl**, which cover a vast range of topics, can help broaden the model's exposure beyond potentially narrow or biased custom datasets. Critically evaluating the data for known biases and potentially using bias detection tools or debiasing techniques during or after training are also important steps.

370

Real-World Example: A team at "FairAI Labs" actively worked to mitigate bias in their language model. They consciously blended datasets from diverse sources— including news articles from multiple global regions, varied literary works, social media conversations (carefully filtered), and balanced demographic representations where possible. Their resulting LLM showed improved fairness and broader contextual understanding compared to models trained on narrower datasets.

Conclusion: Level Up To Make It Happen

And there you have it—your guide to taming the LLM training beast! From navigating hardware limitations and memory constraints with techniques like gradient checkpointing and mixed-precision training, to accelerating progress through distributed training strategies, we've tackled significant challenges. We also addressed crucial training dynamics like overfitting and bias, arming you with practical solutions like regularization and thoughtful data sourcing.

371

Setting up the best environment and employing smart training strategies are foundational to creating powerful and reliable LLMs. These techniques turn potential roadblocks into manageable steps, opening up new possibilities in natural language processing. You don't necessarily need a supercomputer to start—a single capable GPU, access to cloud resources, smart code, and a willingness to experiment and tweak can take you far. Whether you're building a chatbot, a translation tool, or the next groundbreaking AI assistant, these solutions make the journey more achievable. Researchers and startups demonstrate daily that resourcefulness and clever techniques lead to real-world success. So, grab your gear, implement a strategy or two, and unlock your LLM's full potential. You've got this—go conquer that mountain!

CHAPTER 10: LLM Deep Dive: Recap, Resources, and the Road Ahead

Your Launchpad to LLM Greatness

Hey there, congrats on reaching Chapter 10 of LLM - Deep Dive! You've made it through the wild ride of large language models (LLMs)—from the nuts and bolts of hardware and software to the art of training and managing projects. It's been a big journey, and now it's time to take a breath, look back, and gear up for what's next.

This chapter is your launchpad—a recap of the coolest insights, real-world wins, handy resources, and a peek at the road ahead. Think of it like packing your bags after a great trip: we'll gather the best souvenirs (lessons), share a success story, and map out your next adventure. Whether you're a solo tinkerer or dreaming of leading an AI team, you've got the tools to make magic happen. So, let's tie it all together and launch you into your LLM future—ready to roll!

373

10.1 Summary of Key Insights: A Bird's-Eye View

Let's zoom out and recap the big ideas from our journey. Each chapter gave you a piece of the LLM puzzle—here's how they fit together. Let's take a moment to review the key takeaways from each chapter.

10.2 Case Study: NeuralWave Solutions—Innovating Through Limits

Let's spotlight a real-world win to see these ideas in action. NeuralWave Solutions, a scrappy tech startup, faced the classic challenge of training an advanced model with limited hardware. Their story shows how creativity and key insights can conquer the toughest hurdles.

The Challenge

NeuralWave wanted to develop a smart LLM for customer support that could understand tricky questions and provide fast replies. However, they only had a handful of mid-range GPUs—not the high-end data center rigs used by big companies. Memory

374

overflow crashed their early runs, and training took forever. Sound familiar?

The Solutions

1. **Gradient Checkpointing**: They used this memory-saving trick to recompute instead of store everything, significantly reducing memory usage.

2. **bfloat16 Precision**: By switching to lighter numbers (bfloat16), they halved memory use without a significant drop in accuracy, speeding up the process.

3. **Distributed Training**: They spread the workload across their GPUs, turning a solo effort into a team collaboration.

The Win

With these tweaks, NeuralWave trained a powerful LLM in weeks instead of months. This LLM now powers their support bot, handling customer interactions like a pro. They even started selling their LLM to clients, proving

375

that hardware constraints can be outsmarted with clever software tricks.

Key Takeaways

- Hardware constraints? Outsmart them with software tricks.
- Small resources can still achieve big wins with the right approach.

Real-world problems spark real-world solutions—your challenges are your superpower!

Practical Tip: Try Their Playbook

Got a modest GPU? Test gradient checkpointing. It's a game-changer for tight spaces!

376

10.3 Resources for Continued Learning: Your LLM Toolkit

The world of LLMs is constantly evolving, making continuous learning essential. This toolkit provides beginner-friendly resources to help you deepen your understanding and stay current. Choose one resource from each category to test and refine your learning path.

Where to Learn More

Online Courses:

- **Deep Learning Specialization**: A broad introduction to deep learning fundamentals available on Coursera.
- **CS50's AI**: A free and engaging course covering AI basics, offered by HarvardX on edX.
- Fast.ai: Hands-on, practical courses for diving into real-world applications at fast.ai.

Books:

- Goodfellow, I., Bengio, Y., & Courville, A. (2016). *Deep Learning*. MIT Press.

- Bird, S., Klein, E., & Loper, E. (2009). *Natural Language Processing with Python*. O'Reilly Media.
- Jurafsky, D., & Martin, J. H. (2023). *Speech and Language Processing* (3rd ed. Draft).

Research Papers:

- Vaswani, A., Shazeer, N., Parmar, N., Uszkoreit, J., Jones, L., Gomez, A. N., ... & Polosukhin, I. (2017). *Attention is All You Need*. Advances in Neural Information Processing Systems, 30.

- Devlin, J., Chang, M. W., Lee, K., & Toutanova, K. (2018). *BERT: Pre-training of Deep Bidirectional Transformers for Language Understanding*. arXiv preprint arXiv:1810.04805.

- Brown, T. B., Mann, B., Ryder, N., Subbiah, M., Kaplan, J., Dhariwal, P., ... & Amodei, D. (2020). *Language Models are Few-Shot Learners*. Advances in Neural Information Processing Systems, 33, 1877-1901.

Websites & Blogs:

- **Hugging Face Blog**: Articles, tutorials, and news about LLMs and NLP.
- **Papers With Code**: Tracks research papers, benchmarks, and implementations.
- **Distill**: Clear, insightful explanations of machine learning concepts.
- **Social Media & Community:**
- **X (formerly Twitter)**: Follow AI experts for quick tips and insights.
- **LinkedIn**: Connect with industry professionals and participate in discussions.
- **Hugging Face Forums**: A community for discussing LLMs and NLP.
- **Reddit**: Subreddits like r/MachineLearning and r/LanguageTechnology.
- **Discord**: Many servers dedicated to LLMs and NLP. (Search for relevant communities).

By leveraging these resources, you can continue to expand your knowledge and stay ahead in the ever-evolving field of LLMs.

379

10.4 The Road Ahead: What's Next for You and LLMs

You've got the basics down, but the world of LLMs keeps evolving. Let's take a peek at where it's headed and how you can ride the wave. The field of LLMs is rapidly advancing, with new models, techniques, and applications emerging all the time.

Key Future Points

- **Bigger & Better Models**: LLMs are growing in size and capability.
- **Smarter Training**: Innovative techniques are reducing training costs and making models more efficient.
- **Multimodal Magic**: LLMs are being integrated with images and audio, creating more versatile AI systems.
- **Less Data, More Power**: Few-shot and zero-shot learning allow models to perform tasks with minimal training data.
- **Ethics First**: Addressing bias and privacy concerns is a priority, aiming for fairer and safer LLMs.

380

Your Next Steps

- **Experiment with Architectures**: Play around with model sizes and layers. Adjust what you've learned to suit your needs.
- **Optimize Resources**: Set up distributed training using a couple of GPUs. Start small and gradually scale up.
- **Stay Curious**: Follow trends on platforms like X (formerly Twitter) or blogs. New tools and techniques are constantly emerging.
- **Build Something**: Start a mini-project, like a chatbot or a text generator, using a pre-trained model.

10.5 Moving Forward

Larger Models: Researchers are continuously pushing the boundaries of model size. The focus is not only on creating larger models but also on making them more efficient.

More Efficient Training Techniques: New methods are being developed to reduce the computational costs of training LLMs. The goal is to create better models, not just larger ones.

Multimodal Learning: Combining LLMs with other modalities, such as images and audio, to create more powerful AI systems.

Few-Shot and Zero-Shot Learning: These techniques allow LLMs to perform tasks with limited or no training data. It's time to be creative and test the limits of what LLMs can do.

Practical Tip for Action:

- **Experiment with Model Sizes and Layers**: Tailor them to your specific needs. Test some ideas from the chapters you found most interesting.

383

- **Use 2 GPUs for Parallelization**: Start locally to enhance your setup, then focus on distributed training.
- **Stay Updated**: Check out the latest developments on platforms like X or blogs. It's time to level up your skills.

Real-World Inspiration

Think of NeuralWave Solutions—a small shop that created a mini LLM that writes jokes. It's more doable than you think.

The Beginning of Your Next AI Adventure

And here we are—your journey through the LLM - Deep Dive is complete! We've navigated pivotal challenges such as hardware limitations and memory management, and armed you with solutions like gradient checkpointing and distributed training. You've seen how startups like NeuralWave Solutions turned constraints into wins, proving that creativity can overcome any hurdle. From software to project management, you've built a toolbox to train scalable, adaptable LLMs.

384

This isn't the end—it's your beginning. Reflecting on this adventure, it's clear: understanding these components isn't just about fixing problems; it's about sparking innovation. You've got the know-how, resources, and a glimpse of what's coming—now it's up to you. Start small, experiment, and watch your skills soar. Whether it's a chatbot, a translator, or something entirely new, you're ready to build it. Fire up your laptop, dive into that next project, and let's make some AI magic together. You've got this—the LLM world's yours to conquer!

From the very basics of LLMs to training them on high-performance infrastructure, this course has provided a comprehensive overview. Now it is up to you to apply your new knowledge and improve LLMs. By embracing these best practices, you'll have the tools to solve problems and, more importantly, a new way of looking at the world. Throughout this deep dive, it became evident that understanding each section is not just about solving immediate problems but also fostering creativity in approaching model development and

385

optimization. This journey highlighted the importance of adaptability and innovation when navigating the complexities of LLM training. You've gained a solid foundation in the theory and practice of LLMs, and you're well-equipped to tackle a wide range of exciting projects.

So, go forth and explore the endless possibilities of LLMs. Create something amazing!

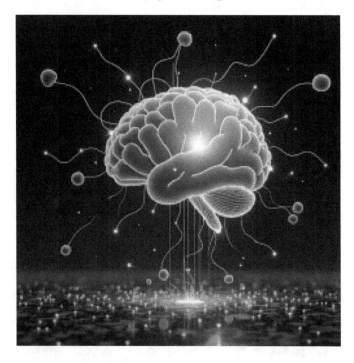

11.0 Chapter Highlights

- **Chapter 1: Introduction to LLMs** - Learned the basics, what an LLM is, and its applications.

- **Chapter 2: The Hardware Foundation** - Explored the components that help LLMs perform their functions.

- **Chapter 3: The Software Infrastructure Behind LLMs** - Discussed how to best build an LLM, including frameworks like PyTorch and TensorFlow. Pre-trained models, such as those from Hugging Face, save time, and smart workflows turn ideas into reality.**Software is the glue that makes LLMs tick.**

- **Chapter 4: Data Acquisition and Management** - Covered data as the fuel for LLMs. High-quality, diverse datasets from places like Kaggle or custom sources power your model. Proper management of data ensures privacy and scalability. **Good data equals great LLMs.**

387

- **Chapter 5: The Training Process** - Training is like a dance—set up your model, feed it data, tweak knobs like learning rate, and watch it learn. Tools like early stopping keep it sharp. **Training is where your LLM comes to life.**

- **Chapter 6: Optimization Techniques** - Discussed ways to speed things up with techniques that make training faster and leaner. **Optimization is your turbo boost.**

- **Chapter 7: Physical Considerations** - Highlighted the importance of hardware, including servers, cooling, and networking to keep your training process running smoothly. **Key Takeaway:** A solid fortress supports your LLM dreams.

- **Chapter 8: Best Practices for Managing Projects** - Organization is key to turning chaos into order. Effective project management ensures a smooth process. **Organization is your secret weapon.**

- **Chapter 9: Challenges and Solutions** - Addressed hardware limits, memory woes, and costs as hurdles—but provided solutions to clear the way. **Every problem has a fix if you're creative.**

Why It Matters

These pieces build a complete picture. It's like baking a cake: you need the recipe (theory), ingredients (data), oven (hardware), and a plan (management) to make it delicious. You've got the full recipe now!

Practical Tip: Quick Recap Cheat Sheet

Jot down one big idea from each chapter on a sticky note and stick them where you work. It's your instant LLM refresher!

With these insights, you have the tools to make your LLM project a success.

12.0 Disclaimer:

This eBook is intended for informational purposes only. The information provided herein is based on the author's knowledge and understanding as of February 2025. The field of large language models is rapidly evolving, and new developments may impact the accuracy or relevance of the content. The author and publisher disclaim any liability for errors or omissions. Readers should consult with experts or conduct further research before implementing any strategies discussed in this eBook. This ebook was written with the assistance of artificial intelligence (AI). While I have made every effort to ensure the accuracy and quality of the content, AI-generated content may contain errors or inaccuracies. The author and publisher are not responsible for any errors or omissions, or for the results obtained from the use of this information. Readers should independently verify any information presented in this ebook before relying on it. Use this information at your own risk.

13.0 References:

- Vaswani, A., Shazeer, N., Parmar, N., Uszkoreit, J., Jones, L., Gomez, A. N., ... & Polosukhin, I. (2017). Attention is All You Need. Advances in Neural Information Processing Systems, 30.

- Devlin, J., Chang, M. W., Lee, K., & Toutanova, K. (2018). BERT: Pre-training of Deep Bidirectional Transformers for Language Understanding. arXiv preprint arXiv:1810.04805.

- Brown, T. B., Mann, B., Ryder, N., Subbiah, M., Kaplan, J., Dhariwal, P., ... & Amodei, D. (2020). Language Models are Few-Shot Learners. Advances in Neural Information Processing Systems, 33, 1877-1901.

- Goodfellow, I., Bengio, Y., & Courville, A. (2016). Deep Learning. MIT Press.

- Bird, S., Klein, E., & Loper, E. (2009). Natural Language Processing with Python. O'Reilly Media.

- Jurafsky, D., & Martin, J. H. (2023). Speech and Language Processing. (3rd ed. draft).

391

14.0 Glossary of Key Terms: LLM Deep Dive

- **Activation Checkpointing (Recomputation):** [187] A memory-saving technique where intermediate activations are recomputed during the backward pass instead of being stored, trading computation for memory.

- **Adam (Adaptive Moment Estimation):** [146] An optimization algorithm that adapts learning rates for each parameter based on estimates of first and second moments, providing efficient and robust parameter updates.

- **Air Cooling:** [27, 155] A cooling method using fans and heatsinks to dissipate heat from components.

- **ALBERT (A Lite BERT):** [190] A model architecture that uses parameter sharing across layers to reduce memory and improve efficiency.

- **Amazon SageMaker:** [22, 64] A comprehensive machine learning platform by AWS for data preparation, model training, and deployment.

- **ASICs (Application-Specific Integrated Circuits):** [14] Custom-designed chips for specific tasks, such as TPUs for machine learning.

392

- **Attention Mechanism:** [6, 98] A core component of Transformer models that allows the model to weigh the importance of different parts of the input sequence when processing information.

- **AWS (Amazon Web Services):** [18, 75] A cloud provider offering a wide range of GPU instances and managed services for machine learning.

- **Azure Machine Learning:** [22] A cloud-based service by Microsoft providing a collaborative environment for building and deploying machine learning models.

- **Back-Translation:** [46, 79] A data augmentation technique where text is translated to another language and then back to the original to create paraphrased versions.

- **Batch Size:** [111, 127] The number of training examples utilized in one iteration of model training.

- **Bayesian Optimization:** [114] A hyperparameter tuning technique that uses probabilistic models to suggest optimal hyperparameters by learning from previous results.

- **BERT (Bidirectional Encoder Representations from Transformers):** [7, 38] A pre-trained language model that processes text bidirectionally to understand context.

393

- **Bias (in LLMs):** [217] When a model's outputs reflect or amplify stereotypes, prejudices, or imbalances present in the training data.

- **bfloat16 (Brain Floating Point 16):** [196] A 16-bit floating-point format that offers a balance between numerical range (similar to float32) and memory savings (like float16), commonly used in mixed-precision training.

- **Branching (Version Control):** [173] A feature in version control systems like Git that allows developers to create separate lines of development to work on features or fixes in isolation.

- **Byte Pair Encoding (BPE):** [44, 78] A subword tokenization algorithm that iteratively merges frequent pairs of characters or character sequences to build a vocabulary.

- **C4 (Colossal Clean Crawled Corpus):** [70] A large, cleaned dataset derived from Common Crawl, used for pre-training LLMs.

- **Cloud Computing:** [18] A flexible framework providing on-demand computing resources (like GPUs, TPUs, storage) over the internet.

394

- **Cloud Storage:** [19, 75] Scalable and durable data storage services offered by cloud providers (e.g., Amazon S3, Google Cloud Storage).

- **Commit Messages:** [177] Descriptive messages accompanying code changes in a version control system, explaining the purpose of the commit.

- **Common Crawl:** [70] A publicly available petabyte-scale archive of web crawl data.

- **Cooling Systems:** [27, 155] Systems (air, liquid, immersion) designed to dissipate heat generated by computing hardware during intensive operations like LLM training.

- **Cost-Sensitive Learning:** [48] A technique to address class imbalance by assigning different misclassification costs to different classes during model training.

- **Cross-Validation:** [210] A technique for assessing how the results of a statistical analysis will generalize to an independent data set.

- **CUDA (Compute Unified Device Architecture):** [16, 95] NVIDIA's parallel computing platform and programming model for general computing on GPUs.

- **Data Augmentation:** [46, 53, 79] Techniques to artificially increase the size and diversity of a training dataset by

395

creating modified copies of existing data or synthetic new data.

- **Data Balancing:** [48] Techniques used to address imbalanced datasets where some classes are overrepresented or underrepresented, to prevent model bias.

- **Data Cleaning:** [43, 78] The process of identifying and correcting or removing errors, inconsistencies, and inaccuracies in datasets.

- **Data Loader:** [23] A utility that efficiently loads data from storage into memory for model training, often in batches.

- **Data Parallelism:** [55, 138, 205] A distributed training strategy where the dataset is split across multiple processing units (e.g., GPUs), each holding a full copy of the model.

- **Data Preprocessing:** [39, 42] The process of transforming raw data into a clean, structured, and suitable format for LLM training, including steps like cleaning, tokenization, and normalization.

- **Deep Learning:** [7] A subfield of machine learning based on artificial neural networks with multiple layers (deep neural networks).

396

- **DeepSpeed:** [61, 63] A deep learning optimization library that makes distributed training and inference easy, efficient, and effective, particularly for large models.

- **Distributed File System:** [24, 76] A file system that manages data storage across a network of machines, like HDFS.

- **Distributed Training:** [55, 201] The process of training a machine learning model across multiple compute devices (GPUs/TPUs) or machines to handle large models and datasets.

- **Documentation (Project):** [179] Written material that accompanies a project, explaining its purpose, design, data, experiments, and usage.

- **Dropout:** [111, 214] A regularization technique where randomly selected neurons are ignored during training to prevent overfitting.

- **Early Stopping:** [210, 214] A regularization technique where training is halted when model performance on a validation set stops improving or starts to degrade.

- **Embedding Layer:** [98] The first layer in many neural network models for NLP, which converts input tokens (e.g., words) into dense vector representations.

- **Ethernet:** [157] A common networking technology used for connecting devices in a local area network.

- **Federated Learning:** [80] A machine learning technique that trains an algorithm across multiple decentralized edge devices or servers holding local data samples, without exchanging them.

- **Few-Shot Learning:** [224] The ability of a model to learn and perform a new task from only a few examples.

- **Fine-Tuning:** [6, 22] The process of adapting a pre-trained LLM to a specific task by further training it on a smaller, task-specific dataset.

- **Flash Attention:** [190] A memory-efficient attention algorithm that processes attention in blocks, reducing memory transfers and speeding up computation.

- **Flax:** [36] A neural network library for JAX designed for flexibility and used for building scalable models.

- **FPGAs (Field-Programmable Gate Arrays):** [14] Integrated circuits that can be configured by a customer or designer after manufacturing, offering hardware customization for specific tasks.

- **Frameworks (Software):** [33] Collections of tools, libraries, and conventions that provide a structure for developing software applications (e.g., PyTorch, TensorFlow for LLMs).

- **GCP (Google Cloud Platform):** [18, 75] Google's suite of cloud computing services, offering TPUs, GPUs, and managed machine learning services.

- **Git:** [93, 170] A distributed version control system used for tracking changes in source code during software development.

- **GitHub:** [93, 170] A web-based platform that provides hosting for software development version control using Git, along with collaboration features.

- **GPT (Generative Pre-trained Transformer):** [7, 38] A family of LLMs developed by OpenAI, known for their strong text generation capabilities.

- **Gradient Accumulation:** [23, 130] A technique where gradients from multiple mini-batches are accumulated before performing a model weight update, effectively simulating a larger batch size to save memory.

- **Gradient Checkpointing:** [187] A memory optimization technique where, instead of storing all intermediate activations for backpropagation, only a subset is stored, and others are recomputed as needed.

399

- **Grid Search:** [112] A hyperparameter tuning technique that exhaustively searches through a manually specified subset of the hyperparameter space.

- **GPUs (Graphics Processing Units):** [10, 16, 152] Specialized electronic circuits designed to rapidly manipulate and alter memory to accelerate the creation of images in a frame buffer intended for output to a display device; widely used for accelerating deep learning computations.

- **Haiku:** [36] A neural network library for JAX from DeepMind, designed for simplicity and composability.

- **HDFS (Hadoop Distributed File System):** [76, 159] A distributed file system designed to run on commodity hardware, providing high-throughput access to application data.

- **Hidden Markov Models (HMMs):** [7] Statistical models used in early NLP for tasks like speech recognition and part-of-speech tagging.

- **High-Speed Interconnects:** [14] Specialized communication links (e.g., NVLink, InfiniBand) that enable fast data transfer between processors (like GPUs) or nodes in a cluster.

400

- **Horovod:** [63, 201] A distributed deep learning training framework for TensorFlow, Keras, PyTorch, and Apache MXNet.

- **Hugging Face Hub:** [37, 222] An online platform hosting a vast collection of pre-trained models, datasets, and tools for machine learning, particularly NLP.

- **Hugging Face Transformers Library:** [34, 95] A popular open-source library providing thousands of pre-trained models for NLP tasks and tools for fine-tuning and using them.

- **Hyperparameter Tuning:** [111] The process of finding the optimal set of hyperparameters (e.g., learning rate, batch size) for a learning algorithm.

- **Hyperparameters:** [10, 111] Configuration variables external to the model whose values are set before the learning process begins, controlling the training process.

- **Immersion Cooling:** [27, 155] A cooling method where hardware components are submerged in a thermally conductive but electrically insulating dielectric liquid.

- **InfiniBand:** [14, 157] A high-performance, low-latency computer networking communications standard used in supercomputers and data centers.

401

- **Initialization (Model):** [100] The process of setting the initial values for the parameters (weights and biases) of a neural network before training.

- **JAX:** [36] A Python library for high-performance numerical computation, particularly machine learning research, combining Autograd and XLA.

- **Jupyter Notebooks:** [92, 179] An open-source web application that allows users to create and share documents containing live code, equations, visualizations, and narrative text.

- **Keras API:** [35] A high-level API for building and training neural networks, often used with TensorFlow.

- **Knowledge Distillation:** [65, 198] A model compression technique where a smaller "student" model is trained to mimic the behavior of a larger, pre-trained "teacher" model.

- **Knowledge Sharing:** [181] The process of disseminating information, insights, and learnings within a team or community.

- **LaMDA (Language Model for Dialogue Applications):** [7] A family of conversational LLMs developed by Google.

402

- **Large Language Models (LLMs):** [6, 229] Advanced artificial intelligence systems trained on vast amounts of text data to understand, generate, and manipulate human language.

- **Learning Rate:** [111] A hyperparameter that controls how much to change the model in response to the estimated error each time the model weights are updated.

- **Lemmatization:** [45, 51] The process of reducing words to their base or dictionary form (lemma).

- **Liquid Cooling:** [27, 155] A cooling method that uses a liquid coolant to transfer heat away from hot components.

- **Llama 2:** [38] A family of open-source LLMs released by Meta.

- **Local Storage:** [76] Data storage directly attached to or within a single computer system, as opposed to network or cloud storage.

- **Long Short-Term Memory (LSTM) Networks:** [7] A type of recurrent neural network (RNN) architecture designed to remember information for long periods.

- **Low-Rank Factorization:** [198] A model compression technique that approximates large weight matrices by decomposing them into smaller, lower-rank matrices.

403

- **Machine Learning (ML):** [7, 229] A field of artificial intelligence that uses statistical techniques to give computer systems the ability to "learn" from data without being explicitly programmed.

- **Memory Management:** [127] Techniques and strategies for efficiently using available memory (especially GPU VRAM) during model training and inference.

- **Microsoft Azure:** [18] Microsoft's cloud computing platform, offering GPU instances and AI services.

- **Mixed-Precision Training:** [134, 196] A technique that uses both 16-bit (e.g., float16 or bfloat16) and 32-bit floating-point numbers during training to speed up computations and reduce memory usage.

- **Model Architecture:** [101] The specific design and structure of a neural network, including the types of layers, their arrangement, and connections.

- **Model Compression:** [198] Techniques to reduce the size (number of parameters or memory footprint) of a machine learning model, such as pruning or quantization.

- **Model Parallelism:** [55, 135, 207] A distributed training strategy where different parts of a large model are placed on different devices (e.g., GPUs) because the entire model doesn't fit on a single device.

- **Multimodal Learning:** [224] An area of machine learning that aims to build models that can process and relate information from multiple types of data (modalities), such as text, images, and audio.

- **Multi-Query Attention (MQA):** [190] An attention mechanism variant where key and value projections are shared across multiple attention heads to reduce KV cache memory.

- **Natural Language Processing (NLP):** [7] A subfield of artificial intelligence concerned with the interaction between computers and humans in natural language.

- **Networking (for LLM Systems):** [157] The infrastructure (hardware and protocols) enabling communication and data transfer between servers and components in an LLM training cluster.

- **Neural Networks:** [6] Computing systems inspired by the biological neural networks that constitute animal brains, used in deep learning.

405

- **Neuromorphic Computing:** [14] Hardware designed to mimic the neuro-biological architectures present in the nervous system.

- **Normalization (Text):** [45, 51] The process of transforming text into a canonical (standard) form, e.g., converting to lowercase, removing punctuation.

- **NVLink:** [14, 16, 157] NVIDIA's high-speed, direct GPU-to-GPU interconnect technology.

- **NVMe SSDs (Non-Volatile Memory Express Solid-State Drives):** [19] High-performance SSDs that use the NVMe protocol for faster data access.

- **Object Storage:** [75, 159] A data storage architecture that manages data as objects, as opposed to a file hierarchy or blocks, often used for large amounts of unstructured data in the cloud.

- **OpenAI:** [70, 154] An artificial intelligence research and deployment company.

- **Optimization (Model Training):** [111] The process of adjusting model parameters and training procedures to minimize a loss function and improve model performance.

- **Optimizer States:** [127] Additional parameters stored by optimizers (like Adam) for each model parameter, such as

406

momentum or adaptive learning rate estimates, contributing to memory usage.

- **Oversampling:** [48] A data balancing technique that increases the number of instances in the minority class.

- **Overfitting:** [210, 214] A modeling error that occurs when a function is too closely fit to a limited set of data points, leading to poor generalization on unseen data.

- **PagedAttention:** [127] An efficient attention mechanism that manages memory for attention caches using virtual memory paging.

- **Parallelization:** [135] Distributing computational tasks across multiple processing units to accelerate execution.

- **Parameters (Model):** [6, 98] The learnable components (weights and biases) of a machine learning model that are adjusted during training.

- **Parameter Sharing:** [190] A technique where the same set of parameters is used in multiple parts of a model to reduce the total parameter count.

- **Pipeline Parallelism:** [61, 201] A type of model parallelism where the model is divided into sequential stages, and data micro-batches flow through these stages across different devices like an assembly line.

407

- **Power Distribution Unit (PDU):** [20, 156] A device with multiple outlets designed to distribute electric power, especially to racks of computers and networking equipment.

- **Power Management:** [20, 155] Strategies and systems for ensuring reliable, efficient, and sufficient power delivery to computing hardware.

- **Power Supply Unit (PSU):** [20, 156] A hardware component that supplies power to the other components in a computer or server.

- **Pre-trained Models:** [36] Machine learning models that have been previously trained on large datasets, often for a general task, and can be fine-tuned for specific applications.

- **Pre-training:** [6, 10] The initial phase of training a large model on a massive, general dataset before fine-tuning it for specific tasks.

- **Pruning (Model):** [198] A model compression technique that involves removing less important weights or connections from a neural network to reduce its size and complexity.

408

- **Pull Requests (PRs):** [170, 175] A feature in version control hosting platforms (like GitHub) where a contributor asks for their changes to be merged into another branch, often triggering code review.

- **PyTorch:** [34, 91] An open-source machine learning framework based on the Torch library, widely used for applications such as computer vision and natural language processing.

- **PyTorch DistributedDataParallel (DDP):** [63, 138, 205] A PyTorch module that enables efficient data parallelism across multiple GPUs or machines.

- **PyTorch Lightning:** [34] A lightweight PyTorch wrapper for high-performance AI research, abstracting away boilerplate training code.

- **Python:** [34, 87] A high-level, interpreted programming language widely used in machine learning and data science.

- **Quantization (Model):** [198] A model compression technique that reduces the precision of model weights and/or activations (e.g., from 32-bit floats to 8-bit integers) to decrease model size and speed up inference.

409

- **QLoRA (Quantized Low-Rank Adaptation):** [190] An efficient fine-tuning technique that uses quantization and low-rank adapters to reduce memory usage.

- **RAID (Redundant Array of Independent Disks):** [158] A data storage virtualization technology that combines multiple physical disk drive components into one or more logical units for data redundancy, performance improvement, or both.

- **RAM (Random Access Memory):** [89, 152, 229] The volatile memory a computer uses to store data that is being actively processed.

- **Random Initialization:** [100] Setting the initial weights of a neural network to small random values.

- **Random Search:** [113] A hyperparameter tuning technique that samples hyperparameter configurations randomly from a defined search space.

- **Recurrent Neural Networks (RNNs):** [7] A class of artificial neural networks where connections between nodes form a directed graph along a temporal sequence, allowing them to process sequential data.

410

- **Redundancy (System):** [158] The duplication of critical components or functions of a system with the intention of increasing reliability.

- **Regularization:** [23, 214] Techniques used to prevent overfitting in machine learning models by adding a penalty to the loss function or constraining model complexity.

- **RMSprop (Root Mean Square Propagation):** [146] An adaptive learning rate optimization algorithm.

- **RoBERTa (Robustly Optimized BERT Pretraining Approach):** [38] A variant of BERT that modifies key hyperparameters and training procedures, leading to improved performance.

- **Scalability:** [18, 81] The capability of a system, network, or process to handle a growing amount of work, or its potential to be enlarged to accommodate that growth.

- **Server Specifications:** [152] The technical details and capabilities of server hardware, including CPU, GPU, RAM, and storage.

- **SMOTE (Synthetic Minority Over-sampling Technique):** [48] An oversampling technique that creates synthetic samples for the minority class to address class imbalance.

411

- **Softmax Activation Function:** [98] An activation function that converts a vector of K real numbers into a probability distribution of K possible outcomes.

- **Sparse Attention:** [190] Attention mechanisms that compute attention over a subset of tokens to improve efficiency for long sequences.

- **SSD (Solid-State Drive):** [19, 89, 229] A type of non-volatile storage media that stores persistent data on solid-state flash memory.

- **Stemming:** [45, 51] A text normalization process of reducing words to their root or stem form.

- **Stochastic Gradient Descent (SGD):** [146] An iterative optimization algorithm used for minimizing a loss function in machine learning.

- **Stop Word Removal:** [45, 51] The process of removing common words (like "the", "is", "in") that often provide little semantic information from text data.

- **Storage Solutions:** [19, 75] Systems and technologies for storing and managing digital data (e.g., SSDs, HDDs, cloud storage).

- **Subword Tokenization:** [44, 78] Tokenization methods (like BPE, WordPiece) that break words into smaller, meaningful units, helping to handle rare words and reduce vocabulary size.

- **Support Vector Machines (SVMs):** [7] Supervised learning models with associated learning algorithms that analyze data for classification and regression analysis.

- **T5 (Text-to-Text Transfer Transformer):** [38] A Transformer model that frames all NLP tasks as a text-to-text problem.

- **Tensor Parallelism:** [61, 201] A type of model parallelism where individual large tensors (like weight matrices) within a model layer are split across multiple devices.

- **Tensor Processing Units (TPUs):** [10, 14, 17, 89, 229] Custom-designed ASICs developed by Google specifically for accelerating machine learning workloads.

- **TensorBoard:** [35] A visualization toolkit for TensorFlow (and compatible with PyTorch) that helps track and visualize metrics such as loss and accuracy, model graphs, and more.

- **TensorFlow:** [35, 91] An open-source machine learning platform developed by Google, widely used for building and deploying ML models.

413

- **TensorFlow Distributed Training:** [63] Functionality within TensorFlow for distributing model training across multiple devices or machines.

- **Text Generation:** [67] The task of producing natural language text by an AI model.

- **Tokenization:** [6, 44, 51, 78] The process of breaking down a sequence of text into smaller units called tokens (e.g., words, subwords, or characters).

- **Tokens:** [6] The basic units of text (words, subwords, characters) that an LLM processes.

- **torchtext:** [34] A PyTorch library that provides utilities for data loading and preprocessing for NLP tasks.

- **Transformer Architecture:** [6, 7, 98] A neural network architecture based on self-attention mechanisms, which has become the foundation for most modern LLMs.

- **Undersampling:** [48] A data balancing technique that reduces the number of instances in the majority class.

- **Universal Transformer Memory:** [190] Advanced memory mechanisms that enable transformers to selectively retain relevant information, reducing memory costs.

414

- **Uninterruptible Power Supply (UPS):** [27, 156] A device that provides emergency power to a load when the input power source fails.

- **Version Control:** [93, 170] A system that records changes to a file or set of files over time so that specific versions can be recalled later.

- **Virtual Environment (Python):** [87] An isolated Python environment that allows packages to be installed for a particular project, rather than globally.

- **VRAM (Video Random Access Memory):** [16] The memory on a graphics card used to store image data and other information processed by the GPU.

- **Web Scraping:** [73] The process of automatically extracting data from websites.

- **Weight Decay:** [214] A regularization technique (L2 regularization) that adds a penalty to the loss function based on the magnitude of model weights to prevent overfitting.

- **WordPiece:** [44] A subword tokenization algorithm similar to BPE, used in models like BERT.

415

- **Xavier Initialization:** [100] A method for initializing the weights of a neural network to help prevent gradients from vanishing or exploding during training.

- **Zero-Shot Learning:** [224] The ability of a model to perform a task without having received any explicit training examples for that specific task.

416

www.ingramcontent.com/pod-product-compliance
Lightning Source LLC
La Vergne TN
LVHW051220050326
832903LV00028B/2182